"Every employee, especially those early in their careers, will benefit from the wisdom in *Y's Up!*, enabling them to get ahead in today's competitive workplace."

Peter Scialdone, Founder, IBC, Inc. (Irvine, CA., USA)

TM

85 *Tips from the Trenches* to Help You Succeed in Today's No-Guarantees Job Market

JAMES J. SIMON & NICOLE D. SIMON

ISBN: 1-4392-3653-4

EAN13: 9781439236536

http://www.TipsFromTheTrenches.info
YsUp@TipsFromTheTrenches.info

To order additional copies, please contact:
BookSurge, LLC
www.booksurge.com
1-866-308-6235
orders@booksurge.com

To Madeline,
who inspires us to be better people each and every day.

TABLE OF CONTENTS

PART II: TIPS FOR OUTSIDE THE OFFICE— HOW EXTRACURRICULAR ACTIVITIES CONTRIBUTE TO YOUR SUCCESS

PART III: TIPS TO MAXIMIZE YOUR JOB SECURITY

ACKNOWLEDGEMENTS

Family, friends, and colleagues have been generous in sharing their knowledge and advice with us over the years. Any information we are able to pass along to you is at least partially a result of their generosity. We thank them for their role in helping us become better managers and businesspeople. The greatest appreciation goes to our parents, who helped us to become what we are today and who continue to influence what we will be tomorrow.

PREFACE

What This Book Will Show You

This book provides tips based on our experiences and the advice we have been given in the business world both domestically and internationally. Our goal in writing this book is to help you *wise up* (hence the title) and be successful.

There is no one way to measure success, since it truly is a subjective concept and best defined by each individual. If, however, your goal is to be better at what you do, then there are attributes of successful people you can adopt. Our advice and opinions can be used specifically in business or generally in life.

Why have we written this book? The concept originated when we were asked to share "tips from the trenches" with university students who were about to embark on their careers. Based on their positive reception, we decided to share our tips with a global audience.

We believe it is important to focus on basic concepts that can really help you while requiring minimum effort. Granted, many of the tips are grounded in common sense, but never underestimate the power or *rarity* of common sense. None of the tips herein were covered in our undergraduate or graduate courses, so they likely will present you with fresh ways of understanding what you can do to change how you act or work to ensure that you excel.

Each tip is its own section, making the tips easy to read in any order, especially if you only have a short amount of time in one sitting. We use "Real-life Examples" to clarify what we mean and to illustrate how a tip may be implemented specifically by you. Each tip section concludes with a "Takeaway," which is a concise summary of the tip. A summary of Takeaways appears toward the end of this book for quick reference.

Although the book is primarily written for Generation Y readers, we recognize that you may be any age and at any stage in your career. In addition, we recognize that you may be (or will be) from any type of organization: large, small, public, private, nonprofit, or family-owned. As such, we refer to your "organization" rather than calling it a company or business. Furthermore, you may be in a mature market like North America or Western Europe or perhaps in a rapidly expanding market like China, India, or Singapore. Our tips translate easily across organizations, job type and status, and markets and cultures.

What This Book Will Not Show You

There are numerous resources on how to write a résumé or curriculum vitae, how to search for a job, how to write a cover letter, and how to prepare for an interview. This book will not address those subjects.

While this book is intended to show you the general principles of success that you can apply in your job once you land it, we have included a bonus section called "Bonus Tip: Insights for Successful Interviews."

Feedback and Additional Information

Visit http://www.TipsFromTheTrenches.info for additional information, to submit suggestions for new tips, or to share experiences that you may want us to include in a future edition.

INTRODUCTION: LET'S BE HONEST

An organization hires you because of what it believes you will provide in terms of your capabilities and likely effectiveness in a particular role. What you deliver is measured as your value to the organization. If you are hired as an entry-level employee, the expectations for your role are less than a director, but the work you are expected to do may lay the groundwork for higher-level employees and, therefore, the organization to be successful.

What is your value to your organization? Your *perceived* value to your organization is directly related to your *responsibilities and the recognition of your contributions,* which ultimately decide your compensation. By applying the Takeaways we provide in the following tips, you can raise your value and, hence, your responsibilities, recognition, and especially your compensation. But first, an honest 360-degree assessment is required. A 360-degree assessment is a way of looking at you from all angles; it is like a mirror for your skills. When undertaken formally (usually by your organization), it can be illuminating. Typically, a 360-degree assessment asks people above, below, and equal to your position, as well as your customers and suppliers, to rate you on a number of factors.

If you had a 360-degree assessment, what are the words that you would hope or expect people to associate with your contributions? Would you expect to be identified as any of the following: expert, intelligent, dependable, responsive, customer-oriented, go-getting, trustworthy, friendly, organized, or promising? How would you feel if you learned you were identified as any of the following: lazy, idiotic, overpaid, foolish, self-centered, sloppy, or underhanded?

The fact is that most people form opinions of you in all types of situations, especially in the workplace. You are not flawless, but with a little bit of self-awareness and effort, you can become the sort of person whom others respect. Respect is what magnifies your likelihood of job success. In turn, success positions you for opportunities, assignments, recognition, and promotions.

Are you familiar with the saying, "You do not have to swim faster than a shark; you only have to swim faster than the other swimmers"? Applied to the workplace, developing yourself in various facets will, over time, make you just a little better than the next guy. However, like becoming more physically fit, you cannot change overnight. But you can make small, easy changes over a period of time. Guess who will be the shark's lunch if you do?

PART I: TIPS FOR INSIDE THE OFFICE

When people in your organization evaluate your contributions, they generally ask the following two simple questions:

1. Are you "good" at your job?
2. Are you a "good person" with whom to work?

Being good at your job means that you are effective and you deliver on the job's responsibilities. Being a good person can mean a variety of things, such as that you are empathetic, easygoing, or work well in teams. We have known numerous people for whom we could answer "yes" for one of the two questions. We have not known many people for whom we could answer "yes" for both.

If you were an executive at an organization, would you prefer that Tanya in Finance be a strong performer at her job but an unpleasant person (perhaps others complain about her lack of team spirit and her bitter attitude)? Or would you prefer that Tanya be considered by many to be the nicest person in the office but the employee whose job performance is underwhelming (perhaps she requires a lot of management because her work is frequently late and inaccurate)?

Most executives prefer a strong performer to a nice person, but with a little self-awareness and effort, you can maximize others' perceptions that you are both.

#1
Master Your Expertise

It may be obvious, but the reason that most people are hired and retained is because they provide skills their organizations need. The skills could be as simple as knowing how to maintain a calendar of appointments or as complex as understanding nuclear physics. What most successful people have in common is that they are *perceived* to be experts *in* or *at* something.

Find something at which you are good or for which you have an aptitude and develop it further. If you have a passion for it, then you are lucky. Many people are good at something or have an aptitude in a subject for which they have no passion. Regardless, find what you are good at and find ways to improve upon your expertise. If you are uncertain what you are good at, ask others what they think, and determine whether there is a commonality among their opinions.

When you read about high-level executives, you often will find that they started in entry-level positions, mastered the job requirements, and were continuously given different and more challenging roles over their careers. Each role that was mastered, and the subsequent growth in capabilities, led to new opportunities.

REAL-LIFE EXAMPLE:

Joseph is a professional business valuator. He is able to calculate the complicated analysis of a business' worth, and he is good at it. He discovered long ago that he has a talent for compiling data, organizing it, analyzing it, and making it understandable to others. Since there is a demand for these services, he developed his talent by attending professional seminars and obtaining certifications, and he has made these services a part of his business offering.

TAKEAWAY:

Find something you are good at, develop it further, and apply it to your career. You become invaluable to your organization when others recognize your expertise.

#2
Be SMART—Plan Your Work and Work Your Plan

Develop a list of SMART objectives with your manager in order to provide a clear measure of how you are expected to contribute to your organization in your job capacity. Agreeing upon objectives will help protect you against unclear expectations and will make it easier for your manager to recognize your achievements. SMART objectives are Specific, Measurable, Attainable, Relevant, and Time-dependent.

The process of creating objectives not only helps define an employee's job scope but also can often lead to strategic consideration of an employee's capabilities. This, in turn, could lead to increased responsibilities, which often are precursors to promotions since the employee's value to the organization will increase.

If your organization does not have a formal system of providing employees stated objectives used for measuring their contributions, then you should proactively work with your manager to determine your objectives. Your manager will likely appreciate your initiative, as it will make your future performance review much more straightforward.

Once you have established objectives, the next step is to set goals for yourself. In this construct, objectives are generally medium- to long-term achievements for which to strive, while goals are short- to medium-term achievements or milestones that support your objectives. This structure often is summarized as "plan your work and work your plan."

REAL-LIFE EXAMPLE:

Kellan creates a quarterly set of objectives to keep him organized and communicate to others that he is focused. He sends out the draft plan to others in his organization who may have a vested interest in his objectives (e.g., superiors, direct reports, and colleagues). Doing this gives the others a chance to comment, which makes them *feel* included. Frankly, most of those who are invited to comment rarely do comment, which means that Kellan's plan has his colleagues' tacit approval and buy-in (see "#15: Getting Buy-In").

Kellan tapes a printout of his plan to the wall next to his desk where it is always at his eye level and within visibility of anyone who comes to his office. He tracks his level of achievement against his objectives using colors green (accomplished or nearly so), yellow (in progress), and red (needs work). Because of his constant awareness of his objectives, green is the most prevalent color on his plan and red is rarely needed.

Kellan also creates short-term goals to support his objectives. For example, to ensure he delivers five hundred qualified leads, he might set supporting goals, such as "successfully exhibit at XYZ trade show" or "post five thousand direct mail pieces."

TAKEAWAY:

Ensure that you are operating against a list of SMART medium- to long-term objectives, and communicate them to those around you to demonstrate your value to your organization. Create short-term SMART goals that will help you achieve your long-term SMART objectives.

#3
Master Your Tasks

Those who consistently develop a set of tasks needed to accomplish their goals are more successful than those who do not. The best way to develop a set of tasks is to keep a task list.

Task lists help you stay organized and in control. There is something especially satisfying about having a list of tasks to accomplish and being able to strike off each task as it is completed, especially as you get closer to accomplishing your goal. Make sure your tasks are doable and able to be accomplished in the time you have budgeted—creating tasks that are impossible to achieve will not advance your goals.

Use whatever format works for you. If you keep a handwritten list or a printed one using word processing or spreadsheet applications, do not be bashful about letting colleagues and your manager see your list of tasks. It is always impressive when someone is quick to take notes of follow-up items. Those who are the most reliable often have long lists of continually updated tasks; these folks add new tasks to their list as quickly as they cross off older ones.

REAL-LIFE EXAMPLE:

To support his goals, Kellan keeps a list of daily tasks on a small piece of notepaper and never allows the list to become longer than the sheet of paper, even though the list often-times exceeds twenty items. He starts a new list at the end of each day in preparation for the following day. In support of the goals Kellan set in "#2: Be SMART—Plan Your Work and Work Your Plan" above, his tasks may include reviewing artistic proposals for the trade show booth, procuring demonstration equipment, or writing direct mail copy.

TAKEAWAY:

Develop a daily list of tasks to focus on and you will increase your productivity toward achieving your goals. Crossing off completed tasks is not only self-satisfying, but it also telegraphs to others that you are a person who knows how to achieve goals.

#4
Sometimes Everything Isn't "A-OK"

When something does not turn out as you planned, do you feel a sense of panic? Worry? Frustration? If you keep in mind that something can go wrong (that is, expect the unexpected), then you will not be caught unprepared. Some aspect of your original plan, no matter how well thought out, might not come to fruition. Ensure your success by thinking a couple steps ahead and having in mind alternatives to accomplishing your tasks or goals. No matter what your plan, always have a plan B and even a plan C for whatever you are working on—tasks, goals, or objectives.

Whether it is having an alternative route to the office in case of bad traffic, sourcing alternative data resources in case your first source does not come through, carrying a backup of your presentation on a USB stick, or having an alternative venue in mind in case bad weather forces your outdoor event to be cancelled, have a plan B and plan C in mind in case something goes wrong.

Murphy's Law reminds us that anything that can go wrong will go wrong, so prepare accordingly. Knowing you have a backup plan can give you great peace of mind and allow you to make a seamless transition in case plans change. Others may not even be aware you are resorting to another plan because you will seem so calm and collected.

REAL-LIFE EXAMPLE:

Anna has responsibility for putting on multi-day events in places like Thailand, India, and the U.S. that include customers and colleagues, sometimes totaling over one hundred people. Naturally, a lot of planning needs to be undertaken to ensure successful events.

One common component of these events is holding an outdoor themed dinner, such as a safari night. The dinner may include food and drink service for everyone, plus entertainment, speeches, presentations, and sometimes even live animals. Having a plan B means that if the weather should unexpectedly take a turn for the worse, everyone involved, from the hotel staff to the event attendees, will easily transition from out-doors to an indoor version of the same event. If done perfectly, most people will assume that plan B was plan A, and Anna's event will have been a success.

TAKEAWAY:

Save yourself from stress by preparing backup plans. Having a plan B and a plan C prevents commonplace setbacks from becoming disasters.

#5
Fact Check and Check Opinions

To maximize your credibility in the workplace, support your opinions and conclusions with facts. An empty conclusion or argument can be easily and quickly disproved and can make you look ill-prepared and uninformed. Your conclusions should be drawn from facts—facts that come in the form of data—rather than your facts being manipulated to support a previously formed argument. It is hard to argue against numbers, and they are easy to understand when presented clearly.

People in the workplace all too often offer their opinions instead of facts. Their experiences have been painful to witness. When a person's opinions are challenged, the person has only three possible choices, which include:

1. admitting his predicament and suggesting that he will follow up with the required data;
2. continuing to speak with the hope that he will outtalk the challenge;
3. arguing his opinion and losing credibility faster than he can imagine as people see through his empty position—the most likely outcome.

Will data sometimes be wrong? Absolutely. Data also evolve over time, so conclusions will have to adapt to the new information. But while the data are current, you should use them to draw conclusions and make arguments. Offering your opinion without having facts to reinforce it is a losing strategy because someone may use facts to disprove your opinion.

Sometimes data are inconclusive, contradictory, or unavailable. When you have an opinion but are unable to substantiate it, your credibility will remain intact if you state your lack of data and why. Your audience will respect your desire for conclusive data and your admission that the data are unavailable. As a result, your listeners will likely give your opinion greater weight.

REAL-LIFE EXAMPLE:

Giovanni's organization marketed a product with a suggested retail price of $229, and he thought both revenues and profits would increase by lowering the price to $199. This was his opinion. He supported his opinion by gathering as much objective and subjective data as possible. Among the things he did was hire a market research firm to conduct end-user surveys to show how much sales would increase with a price drop. He also surveyed his sales team and channel partners for their opinions. A presentation based on thorough research enabled him to confidently state his opinion and earn the trust of his audience, and he ultimately convinced his audience to accept his opinion.

TAKEAWAY:

Arm yourself with data to support your arguments. Even if your arguments do not convince others, you will at least demonstrate your ability to draw conclusions based on underlying data.

#6
Ensure You Are on Time, All the Time

Always be on time. Punctuality shows respect for others and helps you stay organized. Of course, culture has a role to play. It is common to be late in India due to unpredictable traffic. But whether you are in New Delhi or New York, it is common courtesy to be on time.

Leave earlier than necessary to guarantee an on-time or early arrival. Not only will you be more relaxed during your commute, you can use the extra time at your destination to do other work or review your plans for the meeting. With laptops, smart phones, and Wi-Fi Internet access, you can arrive at your destination early and still remain productive by catching up on email while sipping a latte.

What about inside the office? Most everyone is familiar with a colleague or manager who always seems to run late from meeting to meeting. Does this person strike you as someone who is in complete control of his or her responsibilities? There are at least four types of habitually late people inside the office:

1. The poor planner - This person does not have complete control over his or her schedule. Where a meeting might be as productive in forty-five minutes as sixty minutes, this person will allow the meeting to run sixty minutes or longer. Running late makes everyone else late as well.

2. The oblivious - This person is not aware of time-related issues. It may not even dawn upon this person that he or she is late or that the tardiness has affected others.

3. The squeezer - This person tries to get one last email or phone call in before going to a meeting and ends up taking longer than expected.

4. The egomaniac - This is the worst of the four types of late people. This person knows he or she is late and, in fact, relishes that fact. This person may even be following the advice of some business gurus who suggest being late establishes a power position over those who are on time.

Send a strong message about your respect for others by showing up to your meetings—whether in person, via conference call, or via webcast—two or three minutes early.

REAL-LIFE EXAMPLE:

A former finance director rarely made it to meetings on time, even those that he arranged himself. When it came time to schedule a new meeting, he would remark on his busy schedule and how he was unable to find an available time slot. Others began to disparage him outside of his presence—they felt his attitude and his behavior suggested an inflated sense of self-importance, a lack of respect for their time, or that he was incapable of managing his schedule. He had no supporters and eventually left the organization.

TAKEAWAY:

Show respect for others by being on time. Build a cushion into your schedule to ensure that you are on time and as relaxed as possible; you can always use the extra time productively at your destination.

#7
Righting Your Writing Makes an Impact

Because of email and text messaging, an increasing number of interactions these days are done in writing; therefore, the effectiveness of good communications should not be minimized. The original wording of the United States Constitution began "We the delegates…" How different and more inclusive it became when changed to "We the people…"

Write clearly and persuasively to effectively communicate your position and make a positive impression. Poor spelling or grammar may take the focus off your message and damage your credibility. Keep the spell and grammar check application on to highlight any typos you may make so that you can immediately correct them. If you are not sure about something, look it up. There are reference sources online and in print that you can use. You will wish you would of done it. *Note the error?* You should *have* seen it.

Be as concise as possible. As aspiring journalists learn, the fewer words you use to make your point the more impact a message has. You will probably find that the shorter your emails, the better the responses. Remember that those above you have little time to digest details, so you need to process the data and filter the relevant details up. See "#14: Email Etiquette—The Electronic You" for more email tips.

REAL-LIFE EXAMPLE:

Pamela includes her contact info at the bottom of all her emails, yet she often receives a reply asking for her phone number or office address. Pamela knows the reality is that no matter how carefully one crafts an argument, an inattentive reader will not absorb the details. When something is important, Pamela highlights it within her email using font formatting, sparingly. She also starts her emails with her conclusions and if action is required adds "Action Requested" in the subject line to ensure she receives timely and applicable responses to her emails.

TAKEAWAY:

Writing counts significantly—even in an era of emails and text messaging.

#8
Sorta, Kinda Important Tip

Our speaking patterns reveal much about us. The words we choose and how we deliver them influence how others view us. Be firm with your statements and have confidence in what you are saying. Choose your words to convey precisely what you mean. Make sure to enunciate each word. Mumbling over words impairs others' abilities to understand you and makes you sound unsure and lacking in confidence.

There is an interesting pattern of speech in certain parts of the U.S. In what must be an attempt to avoid confrontational language, people at all levels of organizations sorta, kinda insert conditional (non)words unnecessarily into their speech patterns. Words like these make their way into the common vernacular so easily that people may not even be aware that they exist or how they are using them.

Be precise with the words you choose. Have you ever been asked, "Did you want...?" as in, "Did you want to see this file?" or, "Did you want to attend the meeting?" Unless the question is asking about something that happened in the past, the question should be, "Do you want...?"

Enunciate words to show you are confident. Sometimes people slur words or forget to pronounce syllables because they are unsure of what they are saying. If you use a word, make sure you pronounce it correctly and enunciate each syllable clearly. Confidence in one's speech makes a big impact, especially since so many people fail to enunciate clearly or speak precisely.

You may have heard that people react more favorably to positive words than negative. This makes sense. When possible, use positive words in your communications. Instead of pointing out only what is wrong, point out what is right and then suggest improvements. Instead of saying "but," say "and." Simple changes may make a big difference in how others receive your messages.

Eliminating slang or commonly misused words from one's speech can make a tremendous impact by instilling confidence in yourself and providing others another reason to have confidence in you.

REAL-LIFE EXAMPLE:

The following was said in a meeting: "Thank you everyone for coming to my meeting. *I kinda wanted* to go over the results of the promotion. Overall, I think it *sorta* was effective and we should *probably* do it next quarter as well." In print, the words used look ridiculous and diminish the impact of the speaker's reasoning. Audibly, however, the words sound unaffected and normal to a casual listener. An engaged listener will notice. A precise speaker would have said, "Thank you, everyone, for coming to my meeting. We will go over the results of the promotion. Overall, I believe the promotion was effective, and the data support that we should also do it next quarter."

TAKEAWAY:

People respect those who exude confidence, so speak confidently, enunciate carefully, and avoid conditional non-words like *sorta* and *kinda* in your speech.

#9
Now Presenting ... You!

Tip "#19: Selling Isn't Only for Salespeople" purports that everyone is a salesperson, even if one is not employed as a sales professional. At no time is that truer than when one is called upon to make a presentation.

If your presentation skills are not well developed, then your audience may focus more on your delivery than your content. The good news is that learning to present well is much easier than you might imagine. If you are unsure of your skills or if others have remarked on your need for improvement, then practice your presentation skills by joining a presentation group such as Toastmasters, or video-record yourself giving a presentation. Monitor yourself to ensure that you are not using poor grammar, such as "I wanted to tell you," "um," and "ah." Pay attention to your body language, and speak clearly and resolutely. Consider enrolling in a presentation skills course. Your organization may even pay for it and recognize you for showing the initiative.

Do not read your slides or notes. They are intended to help your audience visually follow what you are saying. You can glance at your slides or notes to keep on track, but do not read them point by point or stare at them. Make eye contact with your audience and scan the room. Use hand movements as appropriate. If you give a formal speech, then you can anchor yourself at a podium, but try to walk around the stage. Think about presentations with which you have been impressed; adopt some techniques as your own and practice.

Practice, practice, practice your presentations, especially if presenting is new to you—if this means practicing in front of a mirror at home, then do it. You do not have to memorize each word, but be certain to familiarize yourself with each item so you do not come off as unprepared or uninformed. Do not waste others' time by shuffling through notes.

By the way, do not be alarmed if you see one or two people dozing off. It happens to the best of speakers. Even though it may be rude in some cultures, it does happen, so do not let it unnerve you.

REAL-LIFE EXAMPLE:

Conner attended a two-day presentation skills course early in his career and was able to improve dramatically in that short amount of time. A key factor was watching video play-back of each participant's presentation during which the class critiqued the presenters on many aspects. The feedback from the instructor and other participants was invaluable in sharp-ening Conner's presentation skills and giving him confidence in interpersonal communications as well.

TAKEAWAY:

Becoming a skilled presenter will pay enormous div-idends, even if you do not anticipate having to make a formal presentation. The skills you gain will be in-valuable in formal presentations as well as in your interactions with people on a daily basis.

#10
Empowering Your PowerPoint

You will be called upon to make presentations in any one of a variety of scenarios: a formal speech to a large group, a sales presentation to a prospective client, a budget update to the finance group, or perhaps a department update in a quarterly management meeting. The presentations may be based in notes, slides, or graphs. Whatever format you use, organize your presentation around your audience's needs, and ensure you are making your point as clear and concise as possible.

The most effective presenters organize their presentations around three steps:

1. I will tell you what I am going to tell you.
2. I tell you.
3. I tell you what I told you (i.e., draw conclusions for them as many may have been preoccupied with their BlackBerry® devices, daydreaming, or sleeping).

In all presentations, especially sales presentations in which you are trying to motivate a certain behavior, make sure that you draw conclusions *for* your audience. This ensures they clearly understand your message.

If you use PowerPoint or another presentation software application, as many of us do for presentations, remember to use the rule of three. Always organize one slide around a certain topic or header. For each header, include three sub-headers. Try not to overlook this rule of thumb as doing so may limit the effectiveness of your message and may lead you to stray from your key messages. You may choose to use graphics, but use only those that help prove or illustrate your key messages. Too many graphics can be distracting or unprofessional.

REAL-LIFE EXAMPLE:

Early in Claire's career, a manager showed Claire something that she remembers and implements every day. At the end of each presentation, Claire's manager included a Takeaway Slide that highlighted the main messages from the presentation. The slide also served as a tool when creating the presentation because it forced her to stick to the key points. Since people have a limited attention span, especially in marathon meetings, a Takeaway Slide reinforces the key messages. You can see how much we like this idea, since we have included a Takeaway for each tip!

TAKEAWAY:

Make sure the content of your presentations is memorable by making your content clear, understandable, and easy for your audience to follow. Remember, tell your audience what you are going to tell them, tell them, and then tell them what you told them.

#11
Excel at Excel®

Spreadsheets initially were designed to help people answer "what if" scenarios or hypothetical questions, such as "How will revenues change if I change our pricing from $1.79 to $1.99?" Today, spreadsheet software is commonly used to create basic databases, make lists, model hypotheticals, and, of course, plan financials.

Even if your primary job is not financial planning, you will inevitably receive Excel files as attachments to emails. Do yourself a huge favor and learn to *excel* at Excel. Various tools within the application can make your life easier.

If you use the graphing or formula features of Excel to make handouts or materials for a report, make sure you format correctly. As with grammar, if you provide people sloppy or poorly formatted handouts, your handouts will reflect poorly on you.

You can master Excel by taking online tutorials or going to classes that are dedicated to helping people of all levels improve. Or better yet, ask someone who is good at it to show you some of his or her favorite features.

REAL-LIFE EXAMPLE:

You can use Excel in a variety of ways for business or personal use. From the very basic (Cady uses Excel to track her home inventory) to the very sophisticated (Dieter uses it to track investments in marketing promotions across his region), the features of the application make it useful for a variety of purposes and help you stay organized. In other words, Excel can put you in control of your data.

TAKEAWAY:

Learn to use spreadsheet applications like Excel to make a positive impression by communicating your data with professional-looking reports and graphs.

#12
Time to Closure—Festering Can Mean Failure

Occasionally you may find yourself not wanting to perform a task that is boring, distasteful, or does not fit your expertise. This type of procrastination can sometimes have a positive outcome because more data may become available, you may become energized about the task, or the necessity of the task may decline. But as a general rule, if you allow issues to linger, you will just create stress and more challenges for yourself.

Individuals who address issues as they arise often disallow those issues from festering and growing larger, which ultimately saves time. Moreover, unless you thrive on stress, addressing issues as quickly as possible will enable you to benefit from having less stress as deadlines approach. Probably the best benefit of promptly addressing issues is that it will allow you more options, which allows you more flexibility in your plans B and C. See "#4: Sometimes Everything Isn't 'A-OK.'"

Patience may be a virtue, but excessive patience or being overly patient may actually be a form of procrastination. If you find yourself not wanting to work on something, ask yourself what it is about the task that is unattractive to you and find a way to mediate it. In other words, just get the job done. As soon as the task is assigned, start working on it—in small increments if necessary—to build your enthusiasm for it and make it less distasteful. The sooner you get it done, the sooner it will be over and you will no longer be bothered with it.

Avoid the trap of confusing *action* with *progress*. A person can be very busy and still show nothing for the efforts. This is particularly troublesome when others attempt to convince you that their actions are as good as progress. Know what the desired outcome is for your work—knowing what your goal is will help to motivate you and keep you from having to do unnecessary work. Actions are good, but progress should be your objective.

REAL-LIFE EXAMPLE:

On Tuesday, Helen's manager requested that she create a spreadsheet for delivery on Friday. Helen realized she had several days before the deliverable would be due. Since she was busy with other tasks and was not particularly fond of spreadsheet work, she "forgot" about the request. As Tuesday turned to Wednesday and Wednesday turned to Thursday, she began to lose available time to complete the task. What if an urgent issue had arisen such as a huge report, an important staff meeting, or an illness? What if a person with whom she counted on speaking for key data turned out to be on vacation? What options would she have left herself?

Time management is a matter of prioritizing tasks. Had Helen started her work on Tuesday she would have put herself in a better position to overcome an unforeseen event.

TAKEAWAY:

Do not mistake action for progress. The key to delivering on time is prioritization—ensure you give yourself enough time to accomplish tasks and allow yourself additional options should you need them.

#13
Set the Record Straight

The value of drawing conclusions from data to support your opinions has already been emphasized (see "#5: Fact Check and Check Opinions"). However, what if your data go missing and one day you realize you need them? Uh oh!

Develop a habit of keeping good records so you can free your mind from having to memorize every detail. Good record keeping is not tossing expired invoices, contracts, reports, and meeting notes into a drawer that is conveniently slammed shut. Records are only valuable to you if you can quickly retrieve the exact datum you want when you need it most.

If you have observed an American football game, you may have taken notice of the coaches who pace the sidelines. They hold a playbook that has a plan for just about any type of game condition that can be envisioned. Develop and carry your own type of playbook (whether a spreadsheet file on your computer, data you have emailed to yourself and can access on your BlackBerry®, or just a mental record of specific data points) to gain the confidence that no matter what type of situation arises, you will have the necessary data. This puts you in control of your data and allows you to set the record straight.

Imagine for a moment that you work in a large office in which you may come across a wide range of colleagues, even perhaps the CEO. Envision the CEO asking you some questions in the hallway: "How much of component ABC is shipping from Asia?" "What are the latest sales figures for XYZ partner?" "If we approve the price increase you recommended, how will it impact sales?" Would you be able to answer his or her questions confidently and with data, or would you make up an answer and hope that it was seen as credible? Would you fail to answer at all?

REAL-LIFE EXAMPLE:

In Chet's position, hallway questions range from "What is the total available market for product ABC?" and "What is our discounted channel price for product XYZ?" to "How much did we spend with our top partner last year?" Because he works at a headquarters, the questioners can range from peers to executives. To ensure he is in control of his area of responsibility, he updates his playbook as new information becomes available. By keeping his playbook up to date, he can reel off the numbers quickly and confidently.

TAKEAWAY:

Keep good records and manage your data so you can answer nearly any question that is asked of you. This ability will show you are knowledgeable and in control of your area of responsibility.

#14
Email Etiquette—The Electronic You

The tone of your writing instantly signals to readers your mood or feel-ings toward the readers or subject matter. You may not even be aware you are doing this. Have you ever received an email, letter, or text message that caught you by surprise? Did something the sender had written offend you? Were you left wondering why the writer addressed you the way he or she did? Sometimes tone can be inadvertent, especially as people find quicker ways to write (e.g., shorthand, Short Message Service, etc.).

Since most businesses use email as the official mode of intra- or inter-of-fice communication, here are some best practices to keep in mind when it comes to email:

- Always use a subject line—it enables people to see instantly what you are writing about and makes it easier to search archived mes-sages in the future.
- Limit the number of recipients to just those who require inclu-sion.
- If you need to copy someone else, only use CC and never BCC (see "#30: Don't Be Blind to the Implications of BCC").
- Always address the recipient by name, or if writing to a group, consider addressing the group as "Team."
- Always sign your name at the end (e.g., "Regards, Naomi").
- Try not to use SMS abbreviations in emails—the only possible exceptions are if you are using BlackBerry® or iPhone™ type de-vices to write your emails and are short of time.
- Remember most organization email is subject to subpoena and perhaps subject to long-term storage and eventual public disclo-sure.

Assume that anything you write will remain in existence forever. Now assume that your mother will see anything you write. If you keep these two rules of thumb in mind, you can be confident that you are protecting your reputation and being respectful of others.

REAL-LIFE EXAMPLE:

Recently, two women from a Sydney, Australia law firm were fired after they became involved in a spiteful exchange of emails that started with one woman requesting payment from whomever had taken her sandwich from the refrigerator. Their unprofessional emails (with the rest of the office on copy) soon leaked to competitive law firms and became news in Australia and around the world. The embarrassment they caused their organization pales only to the embarrassment they caused themselves.

TAKEAWAY:

Take a few extra moments to ensure your email communications are polite and respectful, and follow basic rules of professional etiquette.

#15
Getting Buy-In

Make it easy for people to support your work or work initiatives. Ensuring others have a vested interest in a plan usually makes things run more smoothly and prevents difficulties with implementation of the plan. This vested interest is usually obtained prior to implementation and is called "buy-in," which means that the relevant personnel have agreed in concept to something you are going to do.

People like being asked their opinions, but they usually do not have much to suggest. However, if they encounter something that they were not prepared for, the usual immediate response is negative. To ensure that your initiatives are met with positive reactions, or as positive as possible, share your ideas in advance of implementation. You are not asking for permission; rather, you are demonstrating that you realize others have an interest in what you are working on and are extending a professional courtesy to them by seeking their input.

Sharing plans with others does not mean you will implement all or any of their suggestions, but it will give you an idea as to how the larger work population will receive your initiative. By finding out ahead of implementation what criticism you may encounter, you can formulate arguments as to why the initiative must proceed a certain way or incorporate any ideas that may improve upon the plan. At the very least, having a built-in base of support will make it easy for others to adjust once the plan is implemented.

Making changes before a plan is implemented also saves you time and stress. How? Usually, any argument against a plan after implementation will be the same as what you would have heard prior to implementation. By making any necessary adjustments prior to implementation, you can do so with less visibility and on your own schedule.

REAL-LIFE EXAMPLE:

Several departments at a former employer of Alicia's created independent marketing materials. Sales staff relied on these materials to help sell the organization's products. Unfortunately, the sales staff never saw the materials ahead of production. This frequently led to sales staff complaints that the materials were not useful.

Alicia learned one of the best ways to get sales staff on board with her marketing plan was to engage them earlier in the process and ensure they had a vested interest in the plan succeeding. The easiest way to do this was to run planned marketing materials by key sales staff ahead of production. Ironically, the sales staff almost never had changes to suggest. The mere act of engaging the sales staff ahead of time got their buy-in and ensured the materials would be used.

TAKEAWAY:

Save yourself time and stress by getting buy-in ahead of time with relevant people to ensure your plan implementation is smooth and less susceptible to criticism.

#16
Less Is Sometimes More

When communicating with colleagues in either formal or informal situations, ask yourself, "Can I communicate my message in a more concise or effective manner?"

Time is money, and the money that is being spent belongs to your organization. Anything you can do to keep expenses in check will be beneficial in aggregate. So do not waste others' or your precious time by rambling, providing ineffective examples, repeating yourself, or giving extraneous information. Provide the necessary data to reinforce your point and move on.

You may hear people refer to a "thirty thousand foot view." If you have been in a plane, you will understand what this means—you get a broader perspective from that altitude, and the details are not quite as important. Keep this in mind especially if you are ever asked to provide an Executive Summary.

An Executive Summary should be limited to one page and provide only the highest-level points. It is designed with the knowledge that the person reading it has very little time to digest all the supporting details but trusts that the source can provide all the supporting details if called upon.

REAL-LIFE EXAMPLE:

One of Lakshmi's earlier jobs involved sending market alerts to colleagues to keep them abreast of competitive information. She could have just copied and pasted competitors' press releases into an email and sent them on, or with even less effort, just forwarded the press releases from the respective websites. But she knew the team had little time to read full press releases or articles, so she highlighted the most important points (literally with a different color font), and provided bullets with those key points at the beginning of the email. This way, people could quickly grasp the key information and only read the additional information if they had the time or inclination.

TAKEAWAY:

When it comes to communications, respect others' time and your organization's money by honing your messages to the essential information.

#17
Creativity for the Uncreative

One of the fastest ways for you to position yourself for advancement is by using your creativity. Creativity does not have to mean the ability to design art. One can be creative in contemplating the solution to a manufacturing defect, by saving travel expenses, or yes, even by creating a new product. There likely are processes in your job that you think can be improved. It is not easy to approach things always with a fresh perspective, but this is the best way to make good changes. Think of it as being entrepreneurial and taking initiative.

Constantly being creative is not as easy as it sounds because many people lose their passion once they have been in a job for a while. When you are new to a position, be careful not to forget those things that you "would change if you could" as you are adapting to your new workplace. Make notes of those things, and evaluate them after some time to determine if they are worthy of addressing.

Even more important than working on those things you would change is to keep a fresh perspective throughout your career. Force yourself constantly to think about how the big picture can look different and what you can deliver to make it that way.

Many companies have an employee suggestion program. Take advantage of it. Even if your ideas are not ultimately put into action, your creativity will be appreciated. Creativity is often associated with being a problem solver, and it is always better to be thought of as a problem solver than a problem creator or enabler.

Be careful not to confuse creativity with being a know-it-all, or worse, a complainer. Truly creative people propose solutions and are energetic and optimistic. They seek to improve, while complainers are generally unhappy people who are unwilling or unable to solve problems (oftentimes of their own making).

REAL-LIFE EXAMPLE:

It has been published that a global coffee chain has a product line worth several hundred millions of dollars because of one of its front-line employees. Supposedly, this employee experimented with recipes for cold drinks to attract more customers from the nearby beach during warm afternoons when hot coffee was undesirable. His innovation caught the attention of the corporate office and was soon made a standard offering throughout the world.

TAKEAWAY:

Be objective and think creatively about all aspects of your job and your organization. Being a problem solver will ensure your manager will not have to be creative when advocating your next raise or promotion!

#18
A Job Worth Doing Is a Job Worth Doing Well

Try your best in everything you do. It is not worth your while or anyone else's when you undertake a task if you are not going to try your best. Always remember that any job worth doing is a job worth doing as well as possible, given your available time and resources.

Delivering the mediocre is a waste of time—for you, for the person for whom you are doing the work, and for your organization. If your manager has to edit the report you wrote because of grammatical errors or incorrect data, then you have not only created more work for him or her, but you have also made yourself look bad. If you are unsure of your performance, then ask others for their feedback.

Does this mean you should be a perfectionist? Striving for perfection and being a perfectionist are radically different. Since many people do not strive for perfection, their results are mediocre. If you strive for perfection but still come up short, you likely will at least do a good, if not great, job. Perfectionists also do great jobs, but they often end up wasting productivity while trying to ensure that their job is 100 percent perfect versus 98 percent perfect.

Do the best job you can by trying your best, and when you are done, ask yourself whether more can be done. And when you have finished, go back and refine it a bit more. Going one degree beyond stretches you to look critically at your performance and stretches your abilities. Pushing yourself gets easier over time, and it makes you a more valuable asset to your organization.

REAL-LIFE EXAMPLE:

Maddy asked a shoe store clerk if a certain style of shoe was available in her size. The clerk said no. When Maddy asked for clarification as to whether the shoe was not manufactured in her size or if the shoe size was available but not in stock, the clerk responded that the shoe did not come in Maddy's size. Later that morning, Maddy came across the same chain store in another mall and found the shoe in her size! The original clerk could have provided better customer service by doing a quick computer inventory check and providing Maddy a correct answer. Customers encounter situations like this all too frequently—being a shoe store clerk is not a high-paying job, certainly, but there is a minimal effort toward customer service that should be delivered.

TAKEAWAY:

Develop a critical eye for your own work, and try to deliver more than is expected. By delivering quality, above-and-beyond results, you enhance your value to your organization and create a reputation for yourself as one who delivers.

#19
Selling Isn't Only for Salespeople

Each of us is a salesperson whether we know it or not—we each sell ideas every day. Selling is about convincing people of your point of view, and in many cases, getting people to take action to support your goals.

A human resources employee may need to sell his or her manager on the need for an increase in healthcare benefits given healthcare inflation. The manager, in turn, may need to sell the executive committee that the increase in benefits will not only assist employees but also will have a positive effect on the organization's bottom line.

Proper selling is about solving others' wants, needs, and problems. Sometimes the other person is familiar with his or her wants, needs, and problems. Other times, the person needs to be shown that he or she has unmet needs. As a salesperson, strive to determine what it is that the other person is or *should be* interested in buying. If you can pinpoint what his or her wants, needs, and problems actually are, you can offer the correct solution. By offering the correct solution, you not only help solve his or her problems, but you also create goodwill—the most valuable asset of all.

REAL-LIFE EXAMPLE:

Emmeline received feedback from her retail partners that improvements to her organization's distribution processes were needed. Instituting the changes would have a profound effect upon her organization's strategy. After gathering as much data as possible to support her recommendations, Emmeline *sold* the ideas to her organization's management team by presenting the data and her conclusion. Not only were the recommendations accepted, but also the changes that were implemented remain a key differentiator for her organization.

TAKEAWAY:

Developing selling skills, no matter your job description, will benefit you in your job, as you will be better able to convince people to share your point of view.

#20
Can Versus Will

Listen carefully to those around you. When they commit to something, do they say, "Yes, I can do that"? But does that mean they *will*? No, it means something is possible but not committed. When you are committing to something or when someone is committing to do something for you, ensure that *will* is the operative verb.

In addition, be aware of what you promise and ensure that you deliver on your promise. You have no doubt heard that "you should say what you mean and mean what you say." This is good advice. For example, if you promise your manager data for his presentation by Friday's close of business, have it for him or her on time or earlier if possible. If you tell your colleague you will be on his or her conference call, make sure you dial into the call on time.

You may damage your credibility and force others to lose confidence in you if you fail to deliver on your commitments. You would not want to be let down, so do not let others down.

REAL-LIFE EXAMPLE:

Wes has worked with individuals who respond to requests with "I can do that" as a way of closing out a discussion. The inexperienced Wes thought he had succeeded in obtaining agreement for follow through, which allowed him to move to other topics—just what the other individuals were hoping would happen. When the assumed commitments were not fulfilled, Wes learned the hard way that it is important to get someone's firm commitment as to what he or she will do and by when. These experiences enlightened him to monitor his own speech patterns to ensure that he used "will" instead of the less impressive "can."

TAKEAWAY:

Change your can-do attitude into a will-do attitude, and hold others accountable to the same standard.

#21
Open Yourself to This

Have an open door policy. Let your employees and colleagues know they can talk to you by striving to keep your door open—literally and figuratively. A free flow of information is vital to a thriving organization, and having an open door welcomes others to visit and share their ideas. If you close your door for only warranted purposes (e.g., confidential phone calls or meetings), then others will respect that you are indicating your immediate need for privacy.

This rule is not only just for managers who are fortunate enough to have offices. It applies to those with cubicles as well. When people stop by for business discussions, show them that they are welcome. If you are pressed for time or if the discussion veers off the subject of business, then politely inform your colleague. He or she should understand. If you find yourself being targeted by a "Time Vampire," then refer to "#39: Time Vampires—Get More Than You Give."

Showing others that you are willing and available to listen to them shows you are part of the team. Keeping an open door is one way to guarantee you are sending the right message to your colleagues.

REAL-LIFE EXAMPLE:

Manuel is one of the few people in his workplace to have his own office. To make others comfortable approaching him, he makes it a policy always to have his door open unless he is on a sensitive call or in a confidential meeting. If he were to keep his door shut most of the time, then others may assume that he is shutting them out and subtly conveying a position of superiority. Keeping his door open sends a signal to his colleagues that he is there when they need to speak with him. When his door is closed on rare occasions, others understand and respect that he requires privacy.

TAKEAWAY:

Implement and maintain an open door policy, literally and figuratively, to demonstrate your commitment to teamwork and openness to others.

#22
Respect This

Outward respect for others is critical to your success. Do not just say you respect others; push yourself to show others that you value their time, contributions, or efforts. The best way to keep this in mind is always to remember how you would want to be treated, and treat others accordingly. There will be people who treat you shabbily or with disrespect—these people may even play a role in your future at your organization. Understand that we all have people with whom we would rather not deal, but in the workplace, we sometimes have to be the bigger person and not get involved in a tit for tat argument.

It is especially easy to forget that we are dealing with real people when we send emails. Sometimes emails exchanged between colleagues are like missiles deployed across the office. Always be mindful of how the other person may interpret what you have written. See "#14: Email Etiquette—The Electronic You" for more information.

There is no such thing as entitlement or that you automatically deserve something. Remember that everyone is your equal—the CEO, the accounting manager, the delivery-person, and the wait-staff at a restaurant. No one is above or below you. Of course, some colleagues will act as if they are superior to you—act according to your individual circumstances and decide how much you really want to work with someone like that.

Some employers query their reception staff to see how a prospective employee treated them upon arrival. Sometimes individuals, especially those applying for a high-level position, assume a stance of superiority when engaging the reception staff. The belief is that if a potential employee would treat an employer's reception staff in a poor manner, then the person would probably treat others the same way once in a position of authority.

REAL-LIFE EXAMPLE:

We all have encountered people who are nothing less than rude. Keiko, during her first days in a new organization, reviewed a document and put it in the inbox on a colleague's desk as she had been instructed to do. Without comment, the colleague picked up the paper, held it high in the air, walked back to Keiko's desk, and dropped it with disdain. After she politely asked him about his action, he responded that it was not his job to review the document at that point, so he was returning it in that way to send a message. The message he sent was terrible, and it was no surprise (or loss) that shortly thereafter he resigned.

TAKEAWAY:

Show respect for your colleagues, and remember the adage, "What goes around comes around."

#23
You'll Thank Us for This One

Make an effort to say "please" and "thank you" when interacting with others, whether at work or home. If this seems like an incredibly obvious thing to do, then make note of the number of people who actually use these words during the course of a day—not many and not faithfully.

In the workplace, a typical employee interacts with many other people through the course of the day. Remember to be gracious. It does not take much effort to ensure that you use "please" and "thank you" when communicating. When people believe that you are appreciative, they will be much more likely to help you when you need something. Plus, it makes the workplace a lot more pleasant.

Oftentimes, the most pleasant workplaces are those where people are more gracious. Conversely, the most depressing workplaces are those where people have sour expressions and begrudge others' respect. Even if the latter is an effect and not cause of ungracious behavior, an easy way to help stop the cycle and change the workplace for the better is to begin using gracious expressions and really appreciate others for their work.

REAL-LIFE EXAMPLE:

Natalie was at a diner where she asked the server, "May I have the eggs with toast along with an iced tea, please?" The server replied, "Aren't you polite! I wish more people were like you." Having worked in a service position herself, Natalie understood what this server meant. Oftentimes, people get so caught up with their own needs that they forget that the people serving them deserve to be treated politely. If being polite were the standard and not the exception, this server would probably have a more enjoyable work experience.

TAKEAWAY:

Set an example with liberal usage of "please," "thank you," and other gracious words. You will be rewarded with the difference it can make and how others will reciprocate.

#24
A Compliment a Day May Go a Long Way

"An apple a day keeps the doctor away," goes the saying about being proactive about one's health. In the workplace, the phrase might be, "A compliment a day goes a long way." Finding one nice thing to say about and to another person each day is a proactive way of promoting healthy interpersonal relations.

We all have a tendency to see people in a functional manner, such as Fiona from finance, Marcus from manufacturing, and Harold from human resources. We sometimes forget that these are people who, outside of work, are just like our brothers, sisters, neighbors, or friends.

Most people like to receive positive acknowledgment. If you want people to acknowledge you, find an opportunity to acknowledge others first. Smiling is a very good way to start. But you can certainly find something nice to say about the half-dozen or hundreds of people you interact with every day. It could be something like, "Hayley, I saw your report. Nice job!"

Obviously, there is a difference between a genuine compliment and insincere flattery. Be sure you mean what you say, as one earnest compliment has far more impact than a dozen insincere compliments. You will feel better about yourself having made someone else's day, and it may make your workplace a nicer place for everyone.

REAL-LIFE EXAMPLE:

Dylan understands how treating others with respect goes a long way, especially if it means the respect is reciprocated. He likes to remark on a job well done by his colleagues whenever possible. Sometimes the remarks are simple, "You got back to me faster than I expected! I appreciate it." Others appreciate when their efforts are acknowledged. Dylan has noticed that colleagues particularly appreciate compliments after they have made a presentation or have done something outside their comfort zone.

TAKEAWAY:

Complimenting others has a mutually beneficial effect—make your workplace more pleasant by complimenting at least one person each day.

#25
Confidence Counts—Arrogance We Denounce

Confidence makes a huge difference in others' perceptions of your ideas, your work quality, and you as a person. It is easy to notice someone who has confidence. Look at a group of ten people, and you will be able to pick out those who have more confidence. Those with confidence stand straighter and look more commanding. They are well informed, persuasive (possibly without looking like they are trying), willing to defend their positions, and ultimately successful.

It is as easy to spot someone who lacks confidence. He or she may stand with slumped shoulders, stay toward the back of the room, or avoid eye contact. A person lacking confidence may not seem to be particularly knowledgeable, may shy from conversations, or may avoid taking a position. This person may have every reason to be confident because of skill or expertise but talks himself or herself out of being confident. This person may be so shy that he or she does not exert the effort. A person lacking confidence may have an excellent proposal to share with management but tells himself or herself, "I don't think that the executive team will like it. What if they laugh at me?"

So how does one gain confidence? Confidence comes from a lifetime of situations that challenge us to act; the accumulation of successes and failures help build our confidence. A great way to build confidence is to work hard at becoming an expert in your area of responsibility. Others will respect your work, and that, in turn, will build your confidence. Sometimes it helps to have someone who encourages you or believes in you. The problem with this is that there may not always be someone around to believe in you first. You need to be that person—believe in yourself first, and others will believe in you.

Those with confidence need to be aware of the potential of being seen as arrogant. People see overbearing pride or overconfidence as unattractive and difficult to tolerate. Humility is an integral part of healthy confidence. Remind yourself that you cannot possibly know everything, and you will be able to keep yourself in check.

REAL-LIFE EXAMPLE:

Ainsley had a colleague who was her equal in every way, but he had a reputation for being arrogant. This colleague frequently cut Ainsley off when she was speaking. Ainsley could only attribute her colleague's rudeness to his arrogance, and she had enough confidence in her own abilities not to take it anymore. During a meeting between the two of them, when her colleague once again interrupted her, Ainsley pointed out his rudeness. She also said that she respected him enough to let him finish making his points and that she would appreciate it if he would show her the same respect, as her education and experience matched his. He seemed taken aback and never interrupted Ainsley again.

TAKEAWAY:

It may sound cliché, but if you have confidence in yourself, then others will have confidence in you and respect you more, allowing you to be more successful. That is, others will believe in you if you believe in yourself.

#26
There's No Such Thing as Entitlement

No one owes you a job. The world is not always fair. You will not always be recognized for your achievements.

People are turned off when others display entitlement or suggest they deserve a job, salary, perk, or bonus. In the business world, you need to prove that you *will earn* what it is you desire.

Keep in mind that the relationship of employer-employee is one in which the employee promises to deliver certain things, and the employer will compensate the employee for delivering on those promises. That is, you are paid for what you will deliver in the future and not for what you may have done in the past. Furthermore, in some places, employment is completely at will, which means that either party may terminate the agreement at any time further underscoring the fact that there are no guarantees no matter how hard you work.

Because of the way the employer-employee relationship works, there is no entitlement. You could have the most amazing résumé or curriculum vitae, but those documents are only devices to show what you are capable of and do not guarantee what you will do in the future. Likewise, you cannot always refer back to what amazing results you posted one, two, three, or four quarters ago—you need to justify any perks you desire with the promise of future results. When you are no longer able to approach the future with passion or eagerness, then it may be time to look for a job that motivates you to do so.

If you enter any negotiations for jobs, perks, bonuses, or raises with the point of view that you are not entitled in mind, then you will do a better job of convincing your potential or existing employer that you are capable of delivering on your promises. They should be willing to compensate you accordingly.

REAL-LIFE EXAMPLE:

Janae was hiring for an administrative assistant position to help with her product lines. Since it was for an entry-level job, she expected to interview candidates who were very eager to enter the job market and to prove themselves. What Janae found instead were candidates who approached the interview with obvious boredom and no motivation to try to prove themselves worthy of the job. Regretfully, Janae hired a candidate who never seemed to feel that she needed to work hard to prove herself or provide more than "meets objectives" results. It was a disappointing relationship for Janae and probably for the employee.

TAKEAWAY:

Your employer or potential employer does not owe you anything, no matter how successful you have been in the past. Approach all negotiations, whether for a job, a salary raise, a perk, or a bonus, as a matter of proving what you can deliver in the future.

#27
Confidence Is in the Eye of the Beholder

The visual equivalent to a confident handshake is establishing and maintaining eye contact with others. Confident people generally do not hesitate to look others in the eye. In contrast, people with low self-esteem often fail to initiate or maintain eye contact. Not looking someone in the eye may not only suggest lack of confidence, but along with other physical cues it could suggest deceptiveness.

When presenting or delivering a speech, scan the room with your eyes, make eye contact, and hold it for a few moments. Then move on to another person, or find a few people in the room with whom you feel comfortable and alternate among them, making eye contact. Focusing on people prevents you from looking down or reading your materials.

When shaking hands, be sure to look the person in the eye. Eye contact demonstrates that you can be trusted and conveys your openness. Body language experts purport that people who have a difficult time establishing eye contact may be hiding something or acting deceptively. Security agencies even train their agents to observe a person's eye movements as one indicator of a person's misdeeds.

Have you ever been in a staring contest? The first person to blink loses. Staring too pointedly can also make the other person uncomfortable—sometimes this is referred to as a "stalker stare." Be cognizant that you are not staring at people's eyes. The key is to show you are paying attention. If you find yourself staring, blink a little more frequently, or move your focus from the person's nose bridge, to the space between their eyes, to each eye. It may help you become more comfortable with engaging people in the eye.

In some cultures, it is considered rude or aggressive to look someone directly in the eye. Confirm cultural norms before interacting with people from cultures that differ from your own.

REAL-LIFE EXAMPLE:

Cassandra is photosensitive, so she wears sunglasses to keep from squinting. However, she wants to make a good impression when she speaks with people, so she makes sure she removes her sunglasses when engaging in conversations or when having an al fresco lunch. Usually, the other person will notice Cassandra's squinting and suggest she replace her sunglasses, to Cassandra's relief. Cassandra's sister, who has the same photosensitivity, leaves her sunglasses on, which causes visible discomfort to the people with whom she is talking or dining. Not being able to make eye contact with her makes other people think she is hiding something or feels superior to them. Cassandra's approach, although momentarily uncomfortable, is the better one.

TAKEAWAY:

Establish and maintain eye contact with others to show your openness and confidence.

#28

Complainers Are Generally Losers—Adjust Your Attitude

We all know people who are consistently cheerful and optimistic and others who are pessimistic or seemingly depressed. The pessimism may have to do with one's wealth, career, family, or any number of things. To some extent, these factors may be contributory, but studies have shown that lottery winners can be just as distressed as those struggling to make ends meet. In reality, much of our happiness is based on our attitude.

In the workplace, you will likely have colleagues who exhibit a negative disposition. Sometimes sarcasm can be entertaining, and gossip can be informative. But those with a negative disposition rarely are promoted to higher levels. The more negative you are, the less likely you will be a success. Attitudes can be contagious, so if you have many negative colleagues, try to limit your interactions with them. Conversely, optimists are usually more attractive to others as they are more pleasant to work with and usually seek solutions to problems.

You may find fault with processes or disagree with a decision, but try to propose a solution rather than complaining to others. We have all heard that the squeaky wheel gets the grease, but over time, those who complain without proposing constructive alternatives will develop a bad reputation that is detrimental to their careers. Always keep in mind that if you are not part of the solution or do not have suggestions for a solution to the problem, then you may be part of the problem.

Another way of looking at it is if a person has time to complain, then he or she likely is not performing to maximum ability. No one has a perfect life, so focus on what is good in your life and try to have a positive attitude in the office. Accept the good with the bad, and as the song goes, "Accentuate the positive and eliminate the negative."

REAL-LIFE EXAMPLE:

Jack and Jennifer have both had colleagues with negative attitudes. Those colleagues poisoned others with their snide comments and bad attitudes. Although Jack and Jennifer talked to their managers about their colleagues' attitudes, no one seemed to do anything to rectify the situation. Eventually, the colleagues lost their positions during a layoff. The simple fact is that negative people do not succeed in the long term, even if they have short-term success.

TAKEAWAY:

If something bothers you, try to find a way to rectify it. Being proactive about problem solving helps you work better and improves your chances for long-term success. Avoid being labeled a complainer—if this proves too difficult for you, then you will be able to add your lack of advancement to your complaints.

#29
Gossiping Is for Goners

"Did you hear that a decision was made to spin off the ABC division?" "Did you hear that Emma got a 5 percent merit increase, while everyone else got 2 percent?" "Did you know Thaddeus said he was out to dinner in SoHo when he spotted our manager with a mystery woman?"

Interesting? Yes. Titillating? Maybe. There is a reason that magazines and websites devoted to celebrity gossip are immensely popular. But let it be stated here: gossip is for goners. It is like playing Russian roulette. Even if your revolver has five empty chambers and just one filled chamber, the odds are that you will take a bullet someday.

What does that mean? Some people believe that gossip provides the informal communication necessary to navigate rough organizational waters. In some cases that can be true. It may also be a way to connect with colleagues or provide distraction during a stressful day. But when you engage in personal gossip, you are taking a huge, unnecessary, and perhaps unethical risk.

When you participate in gossip, you convey to others that you are disrespectful of the privacy of others. If you are the one sharing gossip, then you telegraph to the others that they might be susceptible to gossip by you. If you listen to gossip, then you show that you are not busy enough. Lastly, if those above you learn of your gossiping, they may rightly begin to distrust you and look for a way to eliminate you from the organization.

It is important to remember that oftentimes information obtained via gossip is mistaken or intentionally wrong. Rather than engaging in gossip, focus on facts and do your job. As with other tips, the reality is that a degree of socializing in the workplace exists and there are attractions to sharing information. However, you should know the difference between fact sharing as a business necessity and being discreet when you learn things that have nothing to do with your job.

REAL-LIFE EXAMPLE:

Geoffrey managed a team inclusive of some members who would be alerted in advance of personnel decisions. Geoffrey could not determine how some people outside his team would know about an imminent hiring when he had only alerted two members of his team. Obviously, one had been gossiping. Geoffrey had his suspicions as to whom the gossiper was, but he could not be sure. To test his theory, he put out an erroneous rumor of his own and was able to determine the gossiper. The person discovered to be the gossiper was reprimanded and was no longer placed in confidence.

TAKEAWAY:

Engaging in gossip can be the start of a slippery slope that could ultimately derail your career—it is best avoided entirely.

#30
Don't Be Blind to the Implications of BCC

Recall from "#29: Gossiping Is for Goners" that if you gossip, you are telegraphing to everyone else who is involved (even those who are sharing with you) that you are indiscreet and distrustful.

The use of blind copying (BCC) in email communications is closely related to gossiping in that it is an act of someone who is distrustful. As a general rule, only use BCC in email communications when you want to protect the email addresses of the recipients as a courtesy. When you use BCC because you want to include someone other than the primary recipient without the primary recipient knowing that someone has been copied, it shows that you are not forthright and, therefore, untrustworthy. The recipient of the BCC may not think of it as a matter of trust, but if he or she sends a "reply all" message, then everyone on the original email will know you sent it to him or her.

Are there exceptions? Of course, there are exceptions to everything. Here is an example in which BCC would be warranted: Assume that a colleague has been harassing you, and after trying to address the problem directly with the colleague, you decide to raise the issue with management (a manager or human resources). As a result, the manager or human resources asks to be BCC'd on future communications. This would certainly be acceptable.

REAL-LIFE EXAMPLE:

Chloe had a colleague who BCC'd her manager on every email she sent. She was not a pleasant person with whom to work, and everyone knew that no matter what was sent to her, her manager would be copied on the response. Since this employee was a bit prickly, email exchanges with her colleagues were often very terse. Whether the colleague copied her manager to ensure others came across as unfavorable, to protect herself, or because she was neurotic, the colleague had a terrible reputation for being underhanded, and people tried to interact with her as little as possible.

TAKEAWAY:

Use BCC only when necessary. If an email is important enough for someone to see it, then he or she should be CC'd. However, use CC sparingly, as not everyone needs to be copied on every email.

#31
Cyberspace—Friend or Foe?

Is cyberspace your friend or foe? The answer to this depends upon what you do online. If you are the type of person who has "unique" interests that you would not (or should not) want to share with others, then cyberspace can certainly be your foe. This is not limited just to visiting certain websites. Blogging or posting to social networking sites can be just as harmful to your career.

For the uninitiated, blogging is when people publish an online version of a diary or journal. Some blogs can be quite innocent and even highly respectable, like those of a person who shares his or her thoughts on local restaurants. But oftentimes, blogs are more like rants that delve into organizational taboos such as religion, politics, sex, and yes, even the workplace (e.g., "My manager is an idiot!").

Assume that anything you publish on the web will be accessible to colleagues, managers, or future employers and could be used as prejudicial information and held against you. A good rule of thumb to follow is if this comes up in a job interview, would you be embarrassed or able to defend it?

Another potential cyberspace foe is posting your profile details on job hunting or matchmaking web sites. Imagine how you would feel if you found that one of your employees appeared to be hanging the "for hire" sign online? Or imagine if you found out that your manager, who you had up until now respected, was seeking group "get-togethers" (a CEO was just caught doing this, and it was splashed across the news worldwide).

Hackers can compromise data that you may think is confidential, so be very careful about what you post. Even if you delete things from the Internet, such as removing a picture or blog post, doing so does not guarantee that it will be erased from cyberspace. Far from it—your twenty-something posts may be accessible well into your forties or fifties or longer.

REAL-LIFE EXAMPLE:

In interviewing a potential new manager, Tran did an online search to learn more about the candidate's professional past. This was in the early days of social networking websites, but he found some posts the candidate had made with some very specific references to her high school experiences. When Tran broke the ice by asking about her favorite high school teacher by name, the candidate was momentarily befuddled but bemused. Now think about whether posting photos of you at a nightclub last week is a good idea...

TAKEAWAY:

If anything you post online would come as an embarrassment to you if your colleagues found out or confronted you with it, then consider not posting, and forgo any possibility of being embarrassed.

#32
The Joke Could Be on You

Did you hear the joke about the preschool teacher and the...? You and your friends might believe that you are a great amateur stand-up comedian, but in the office, seemingly innocuous jokes can have unexpected repercussions. What you may not know is that someone overhearing the joke has a husband who teaches preschool...

In addition to inappropriate joking, injecting excessive humor in your presentations and daily interactions may also have unintended consequences. Excessive humor may lead people to believe you are a goofball and do not take your work seriously. Examples of humor include one-liners, irony, self-deprecation, or teasing. Using humor can lighten a mood or break the ice, but excessive use of it can be irritating or offensive. If humor is part of your personality, then use it where it will be effective—at the beginning of presentations, for example.

Humor becomes offensive when it is at another's expense. Never make others the focus of your joking. If you find the need to inject humor, only do it at your expense and not others'. Self-deprecation is the best form of humor in the workplace, but be careful not to do it so often that you generate doubt about your skills.

REAL-LIFE EXAMPLE:

Winston has worked with a number of colleagues who chose to keep their sexual orientation private. Only after a substantial period of trust had developed did these colleagues share their orientation in confidence. Unfortunately, these colleagues were repeatedly subjected to jokes that obviously would not have been made if the jokers had known their colleagues' orientation. The simple fact is that an upstanding individual would never make a joke about any group of people, whether or not he or she is part of that group.

TAKEAWAY:

Humor can relieve stressful situations and lighten the monotony of a day. Use it with discretion to avoid seeming flip and unintentionally offending or hurting the feelings of colleagues.

#33
Speed We Plead

How do you prioritize requests that come from other people? The answer to that question depends on many variables such as your organization's culture, the requestor, the nature of the request itself, and your available time.

Assuming all things are equal, each request made of you should be processed and the results delivered in a timely manner. Do not procrastinate with things that may be of importance to others. Though you may not understand how important it is to the other person, this does not mean that it is not vital to achieving his or her and your organization's goals. It is a simple matter of treating others the way you would want to be treated and understanding what is urgent and what is less urgent.

If a request is made of you and no timeframe is given for your response, then ask when a response is desired. If the deadline is not realistic, then find one that is mutually acceptable. Oftentimes, a slower, well-thought response is preferable to a lightning-quick, poorly constructed one. Do a quality job within the time specified.

Strive to be responsive. If you are prompt to respond, then you will likely be characterized as someone who is dependable. Dependable people are the ones who are given the most important projects and ultimately the ones who earn promotions.

REAL-LIFE EXAMPLE:

Faye's colleague emailed her a request to prepare some data for presentation to the Board. The colleague gave her a deadline of two days. Faye knew the Board meeting would occur in three days, so she knew her colleague would prefer to have the data sooner rather than later but did not want to encroach on Faye's priorities. Instead of putting off her colleague's request, Faye worked on it immediately and got the data to her colleague by the end of that day. Although Faye then had to take home her own work that evening, she knew her helpfulness would be noted and that one day her colleague would return the favor.

TAKEAWAY:

Treat requests for assistance from others with the same respect and attention to which you would want yours to be treated. Delivering quality in a speedy manner is a fast way to increase your value.

#34
Don't Fear Failure

Everyone fails. Even the most successful people and companies have failures now and then. The most successful people or companies, however, do not dwell on the failure. They process what happened and then move on as quickly as possible. Dwelling on a failure for longer than the time it takes to understand how it happened does not accomplish anything and, even worse, can hurt your self-confidence. The best you can do is pick yourself up, dust yourself off, learn from what happened, and move on.

Failure is really just a mindset—think of it as an opportunity to learn something and apply it to your future. If you try your very best with the resources you are given, then you can be proud of what you have done even if the outcome is not what you desired. The key, though, is to try your best. If you do that, then you cannot be faulted.

Remember, no one is likely keeping track of your failures, except perhaps you. Accept that failure is inevitable, but still try your very best; this is the best remedy for objectively processing any failures and being able to move quickly on from them.

REAL-LIFE EXAMPLE:

Donald Trump is well-known for having had spectacular successes and spectacular failures. These are the result of his willingness to take risks. If he were not prepared to take the bad with the good and move on from his failures, then he would not be as successful as he is today—some say more successful than at any other time in his career.

TAKEAWAY:

Failure is bound to happen, but always try your very best with the resources you have. Embrace every failure as a learning opportunity, and apply what you have learned toward achieving your next success.

#35
Consider Sales

Sales revenue is necessary to a for-profit organization's existence—if revenue is not coming in the door, then there is no business. For this reason, salespeople often are given a significant amount of credit for an organization's success—and sometimes failure. Salespeople may even have perks that are not available to others who may work just as hard. Those who are not in sales often are left wondering why the contributions of non-salespeople are seemingly not appreciated as highly.

To use a football analogy, many in the organization move the product down the field until it is on the goal line. The sales team then carries the product into the end zone, and the organization celebrates the final play by sales, overlooking the key contributions by engineering, manufacturing, quality, finance, marketing, human resources, etc.

Is this fair? It does not matter. If a person wants to receive the same praise as a salesperson, then he or she should rise to the challenge and deliver the unique skills that successful salespeople possess. When non-salespeople complain, "Why do salespeople get all of the credit?" or "Why do salespeople get incentive trips for doing their job?" they have to remember that it is just how sales works. Anyone who wants the perks should be willing to work for them. If you are dissatisfied with doing work that receives little credit, then you should consider testing your skills in a sales role. And if you are not willing to do this, then you should not complain.

REAL-LIFE EXAMPLE:

At Olivia's organization, her sales operations team is usually left processing orders during the last minutes of each quarter as salespeople try extra hard to reach their numbers. This last-minute push generally creates stress and overtime for Olivia and her colleagues. Little or no thanks are given for their help as they process the orders so the members of the sales team can get their commissions. While this seems unfair, the salespeople are working hard with customers to convince them to put in their orders. Although the people skills of salespeople help them with selling, it does not mean they always are gracious with colleagues who help in getting the orders processed. Olivia has occasionally asked the salespeople to take her team out to lunch in appreciation, something the salespeople are generally fast to do once they are reminded of the work others have done for them.

TAKEAWAY:

Salespeople often seem to get all the credit and extra perks. Although it does not seem fair to non-sales, non-commissioned personnel, salespeople possess unique skills that require incentives and are critical to an organization's existence.

#36
Clutch Hitters Win Games

Are you familiar with the term "Clutch Hitter"? If not, it is a baseball reference and refers to the *go-to* person in an organization. You can always go to this person when a job needs to be completed, and as such, this person is highly valued by the organization.

You may have heard the saying, "When you need a task completed, you should assign it to the busiest person." Some people just know how to accomplish the tasks that are set before them, either inherently or because of practice. When a superior needs something done properly, quickly, or sometimes secretly, it pays to be the Clutch Hitter. Oftentimes, these requests are for challenges that are not directly tied to the employee's job description. The fact that a person would be chosen for such an assignment is a sign of respect and confidence.

Becoming a Clutch Hitter often takes time—good reputations take longer than one day to develop. To become a Clutch Hitter, start by being the best that you can be in your current area of responsibility. Communicate to your manager that he or she can count on you when something needs to be done properly and on time. He or she will appreciate your offer, and if you are good at what you were hired to do, then your manager will likely start giving you more opportunities to contribute. Volunteer for additional tasks that fit in with your capabilities and workload. As you consistently demonstrate your ability to accomplish stretch tasks (tasks that stretch your capabilities), you will prove your ability to take on a greater role.

In other instances, an emergency may present an opportunity for you to become a Clutch Hitter. For example, your superior may be traveling on business when an unanticipated task arises to which he or she is unable to attend. He or she may deputize you to accomplish the task on his or her behalf.

REAL-LIFE EXAMPLE:

Alim was an assistant product manager responsible for marketing an existing product in international markets. He had tried over time to prove himself a Clutch Hitter. When a senior product manager who had responsibility for developing new products at Alim's organization resigned, Alim's manager was left with an open position that needed to be filled immediately. Alim was asked if he would be willing to change jobs and move to another state to fill the vacancy. Because he had demonstrated in the past that he was a Clutch Hitter, his manager offered him the job. The move involved an increase in pay and substantially greater responsibility. Alim could not pass up the opportunity. Alim, yet again, proved himself a Clutch Hitter when an emergency arose.

TAKEAWAY:

Be someone that others can count on and earn a reputation as a Clutch Hitter. By helping others, especially your managers, be more successful, you will be the one others turn to when they need something done properly, quickly, or secretly.

#37
Master the Halo Effect

Have you ever noticed that someone who seems to be knowledgeable in one area seems to be credited as knowledgeable in other areas? People who have a reputation for being accomplished at one thing are frequently assumed to be good at many things. Sometimes this perception is warranted, and other times it is due to the Halo Effect.

The Halo Effect can benefit you if you are the one to whom the additional expertise or accomplishments are attributed. However, the Halo Effect can work against you. Assume you have a colleague who has equal responsibilities to yours. If this colleague has garnered respect for an accomplishment outside the office—for example, he or she teaches CPR classes on weekends—then the Halo Effect may make this person rise above you in reputation.

If you have skills outside the workplace, do not be afraid to mention them casually to others in the workplace, especially your manager. Be mindful, though, that what impresses you may not necessarily impress others. Generally, the more a manager knows about his or her employee, the more likely he or she is to trust and mentor that employee. As you become more accomplished at a variety of things, you should let others know how you would like to use your skills in the workplace, which may open you to new opportunities.

REAL-LIFE EXAMPLE:

George's first job after university was at a well-known Japanese organization at one of their California offices. On his second day, George overheard his new manager talking golf with another Japanese manager. When George suggested that he and his manager hit the links some day, he was invited to join in the organization's tournament *that weekend*. When George showed up at the golf course, he discovered that there were thirty-five participants and he was the only non-Japanese player. George was a decent golfer, but that day he played far better than his average (shooting a gross eighty-one, for those who know golf) and won the tournament. Because of the Halo Effect, George was no longer just another local employee, he was "George-san, the golfer in marketing," and additional opportunities opened up to him, including an eventual coveted assignment at the organization's U.S. headquarters.

TAKEAWAY:

Leverage your accomplishments in other fields, and let the Halo Effect enhance the perception people have of you in your work position.

#38
Meetings Often Miss the Mark

The concept of meetings is good: get key people together to inform, persuade, or discuss issues of importance. Discussions can be an important step in solving problems by allowing competing ideas to be evaluated. However, meetings often top lists of unproductive activities.

When you must attend a meeting, do what you can to ensure it is properly managed. A properly managed meeting has a clearly established purpose; attendees are allowed to voice their positions; long-winded, off-base discussions are terminated; and a summary of conclusions (with action items if appropriate) is reviewed to ensure everyone is in agreement.

Running meetings more efficiently results in making them more effective. Aim to continually cut the length of time a meeting takes, especially those meetings that occur regularly. It is common for "meeting fatigue" to develop for regularly scheduled meetings, so making changes to the format can keep participants interested.

When concluding a meeting or discussion, refer to your notes to clarify what each person's follow-up items are. This can often be the most important few seconds of an entire meeting. If tasks have yet to be assigned, your list of action items can be read aloud and assignments made accordingly.

If you are fortunate enough to have others who share your desire for efficient meetings, then have them rate the meeting afterward on a scale of one to ten in areas like efficiency, coverage of content, and action plans. If the results show that the meeting rates low in any of the factors, then the meeting needs to be retooled or reconsidered.

If you are invited to a meeting that you believe does not require your attendance, ask instead to provide your input via email and seek the outcome later (and any actionable items with which you have been tasked). Use your time for more productive activities. If you are the meeting coordinator, then ensure you are only inviting those who truly need to attend.

REAL-LIFE EXAMPLE:

Diane has a weekly meeting with international managers, during which each manager gives an update on his or her area. With a loose structure, the meetings are very inefficient and oftentimes run late with people discussing topics not planned. Diane now sends out an agenda ahead of time and asks for input on agenda items before the meeting. The meetings now usually run shorter than planned, and people pay more attention to the discussion because they realize their time is not being wasted.

TAKEAWAY:

Meetings are often unnecessary or badly managed, but with minimal effort, you can minimize their impact on your schedule and maximize their effectiveness so that you can achieve your objectives.

#39
Time Vampires—Get More Than You Give

Time Vampires waste your time. They may do this in person, by telephone, by email, or by some other means. Have you ever thought to yourself of someone, "Just get to the point"? This person was likely a Time Vampire—one who sucks your time, resulting in you not having enough time to do what you need and causing you to work overtime, rush, or be late.

Sometimes you may not even realize the person is a Time Vampire. Perhaps he or she just wants to catch up on the latest sports score or talk about weekend plans, but if you have better things to do (and you should considering that you are at work), repeated intrusions on your time result in declines in your productivity.

A Time Vampire typically strikes in the following places:

- your workspace;
- a common area (e.g., break room);
- a meeting.

Why are some people Time Vampires? The workplace is a melting pot! Seriously, these people often do not have enough work of their own or at least do not have a good work ethic. They are also selfish since they impose themselves on you. Even if a Time Vampire is a nice guy or gal, you must maintain control of your time.

Realistically, socializing at work helps build relationships, but Time Vampires do not respect your time. The best way to deal with a Time Vampire is to, as tactfully as possible, point out how his or her behavior affects your performance. You can sympathize with his or her desire to converse, but explain that you will not be able to finish your task. When the Time Vampire realizes that he or she is part of the problem, he or she will likely go bite someone else. If you are in a meeting, the best way to deal with a Time Vampire is to follow optimal meeting behaviors. See "#38: Meetings Often Miss the Mark."

REAL-LIFE EXAMPLE:

It is especially hard to avoid Time Vampires when you are in a cubicle. Fiona used to have a colleague who would, as soon as she had poured herself a cup of coffee, come over to Fiona's cubicle and lean against the entry. Even if Fiona were on the phone or in the midst of composing an email, the woman would start talking about the terrible commute or issues with her landlord. If you think the fact that Fiona was on the phone was hint enough that she was too busy to chat, think again. Fiona had to inform her colleague that the mornings are a busy time for her, and she needed to keep her top priority contacting customers.

TAKEAWAY:

Be aware of Time Vampires, as they may suck away your productivity and make you look underworked or unprofessional.

#40
Admitting Mistakes Is No Mistake

Mistakes happen. They happen all the time and to everyone. An honest person will voluntarily admit his or her mistakes and do so as soon as possible after a mistake occurs. Public relations companies invest a lot of time teaching companies and their spokespeople the benefit of admitting fault in a crisis for a very simple reason: the truth rarely remains hidden for long. The longer you keep a mistake hidden, the worse the final effect.

Most people will respect you for being honest and forthright and drop the issue. Pride is a powerful tool, but it also can prevent a person from admitting to mistakes. Swallow your pride, admit the mistake, and you will be able to move on. Once the mistake is corrected, it is most likely not going to be brought up again, as someone else's mistake will require attention. Your organization employs you for your contributions in the present and future. Admitting your mistake will allow you to focus on the future; whatever problems may have occurred are in the past.

There is something even worse than not acknowledging a mistake—trying to cover it up. In other words, you should never lie. If you have a conscience, you will not be able to live with knowing that you lied.

REAL-LIFE EXAMPLE:

Valerie was responsible for overseeing her department's budget. She reported mid-quarter that spending was within expectations, only to realize later that she forgot to include a recent expense that would have put her over budget. She had a choice: proactively report the mistake, or conceal the information and risk having it come out in a top-down audit. The latter scenario not only would have embarrassed Valerie's manager, but it also would have made Valerie look like she did not have command over her area of responsibility. If it could be proven that Valerie knew of the overspend, then she would have diminished her credibility—a triple whammy. Valerie, of course, reported the mistake.

TAKEAWAY:

When you admit to a mistake, preferably sooner rather than later, you are actually building trust in you and possibly keeping your organization from suffering worse effects had you kept the mistake concealed.

#41
To Tell the Truth, Integrity Matters

Your integrity is easy to ruin and difficult to rebuild. If you damage your integrity, you essentially become bankrupt as a person, and your colleagues, especially your managers, will have great difficulty trusting you with greater responsibility.

A person who is dishonest in the workplace will eventually be found out and made to compensate for whatever damage he or she has caused. If Josephine takes extra pens home from the office or Clyde makes long-distance calls to his girlfriend, the budget will reflect their deeds or someone will be witness. Yes, even things seemingly as innocuous as these are matters of integrity. Sometimes it may seem as if someone is "getting away" with something he or she should not, but the luck of a colleague who has been getting away with dishonest behavior for years will not hold up. As the expression goes, "The higher up he climbs, the harder his fall will be."

Perhaps the best way to ensure that you maintain your integrity is always to consider your organization as your own personal business. That is, always ask yourself if you were the owner and all expenses or revenue hit your pocketbook, how would you feel about the action you are about to take? Josephine and Clyde may have reconsidered their actions had they thought about them from this perspective.

Allow your integrity to serve you well. It will provide you mental insurance and give you confidence that you are making ethical decisions.

REAL-LIFE EXAMPLE:

A first-class cabin flight attendant was recently caught taking a bottle of Dom Pérignon champagne from his plane after touchdown in London. The bottle was worth about US$150, and the fact that he took it from his employer made it an issue of embezzlement. His employer had little choice but to fire him in order to demonstrate that integrity is critical. Compounding the difficulty of losing his job, the former flight attendant now may have to explain to prospective employers why he was terminated from his previous job.

TAKEAWAY:

Your integrity is vital to your success and one asset that cannot be destroyed by others—only you can damage it. Be truthful and protect your integrity.

#42

Loose Lips Sink Ships—Learn to Keep Secrets

As you rise in your organization, you will become privy to ever-increasing amounts of confidential information. Most of the information within a business will be classified as confidential to outsiders, whether publicly- or privately-held.

Your organization asks you to keep information confidential for a reason. It may have to do with government regulation or employee privacy or be a matter of corporate competitiveness. Your employment contract most likely legally binds you to confidentiality.

Granted, it can be difficult if you come across information that affects colleagues whom you regard as friends. You look out for your friends and expect them to look out for you too, right? What if you learn that your friend will be affected by a not yet announced layoff? Would it be right to hint to him that he should consider an unsolicited job offer he received from another organization and shared with you in confidence?

Your organization expects you to keep information to which you become privy confidential. If you think of the organization as a person who trusts and honors your integrity, would you want to let that person down by sharing his or her secrets? Moreover, you have an ethical and legal responsibility to keep confidential information confidential.

REAL-LIFE EXAMPLE:

Alfonso has served on several task forces that dealt with organizational-confidential information, like spinning off a division. The actions of the task forces affected many parties, including colleagues, investors, and even competitors. While Alfonso operated under a confidentiality clause, he nevertheless had to sign project-specific confidentiality statements to ensure that he understood the responsibilities to which he was agreeing.

Many colleagues who were also friends began to suspect that something was astir and began to ask Alfonso questions about what he might know. They played up their friendship by promising not to tell anyone if he confided in them. Alfonso kept the information confidential, as he was obligated. As difficult as it may be, the only thing to say is, "As my friend, you'll understand me when I say that it is improper for me to confirm or deny any rumors that you may have heard."

TAKEAWAY:

Keep organization secrets secret. As you advance in your organization, you will be trusted with increasing amounts of confidential information that you have an ethical duty to keep confidential.

#43
Your Verbal Calling Cards

Have you ever called someone and heard an unenthusiastic greeting, live or recorded? Did the person impress you with a feeling of someone who is passionate about doing the best job possible? Did you feel better after having heard the person's voice, or worse?

Be enthusiastic when you answer the phone or leave a recorded message. An easy way to do this is to smile while you are talking; you will be amazed with how it changes your tone. It does not cost you anything but time, and it will leave a positive impression on people. When you pick up your phone in person, a simple, "Good afternoon, this is Cecily. May I help you?" should be sufficient. If you can inject your organization's name, this is even better.

When people reach your voicemail it is a good idea to set an expectation of when you will be able to get back to the person. In a cheerful demeanor, a simple, "This is Edward. Your call is important to me. Please leave your message, and I will return your call within one business day," makes a positive impression.

Many people have a BlackBerry®, iPhone™, or other remote email devices. You can provide your additional contact information on your voicemail message to give callers an alternate way of reaching you, for example, "…or you may reach me via email by writing to me at YsUp@TipsFromTheTrenches. info."

Email itself has become so real-time for many people today that they expect prompt replies. If you are going to be out of reach you should, just as with your voicemail, create an auto-reply message stating that you are away but will endeavor to respond within one business day.

REAL-LIFE EXAMPLE:

Hannah likes to use her voicemail message to advertise whatever promotion is current. "Hi, you've reached Hannah of XYZ Organization. I'm not able to take your call right now. Please leave a message, and I'll return your call within one business day. And don't forget to check out our summer promotions valid through August 31st. Visit www.xyz.com for more information. Thank you for calling and have a great day."

TAKEAWAY:

A bit of verbal pleasantry costs little but is invaluable. Let people know through your tone that they are important to you. Advise them if you are traveling, and state a goal of responding within one business day—and do it.

#44

Funnily Enough, Teams Only Succeed Through Teamwork

No one ever gets fired for managing the winning team. This is a valuable bit of insight and means that when you are part of a team, everyone will share in any successes. As an individual contributor, you should always consider yourself as part of a team and work toward achieving the team's goals. If you are a manager, then it also means that you need to ensure everyone on your team is credited for successes.

Have you ever had a manager take credit for your successes but quickly lay blame on you for failures, even those not of your doing? Did you enjoy working for that manager? Probably not. Be assured, you are not the first one to have that experience, and unfortunately, you are not the last.

As an individual contributor, make an effort to be a team player by focusing on achieving team success. Your colleagues will appreciate and reciprocate your efforts. When it comes time for 360-degree reviews (see "Introduction: Let's Be Honest"), you will get a much higher evaluation from colleagues who see you as a team member.

As a manager, ensure your employees feel they are part of a team. Be conscious of the fact that no one person's efforts are exclusive to others', and everyone has a claim to successes. If the team wins, then assign the win to the team. Should the team lose, take the blame yourself. Why? Because it is the right thing to do. It is important to be generous in sharing success and be gracious in taking blame. Over time, your team members will go to extraordinary lengths to help the team succeed, knowing they will win when the team wins and be protected when the team loses. Unfortunately, few managers practice this behavior; thus, by doing so you will stand out.

When it comes time to recruit people for a new project, you will have the best and the brightest seeking to join your team, which only further enhances your chances of winning. This often is exhibited at the collegiate sports level—schools with a history of success have a much easier time recruiting the best to their team, which, in turn, perpetuates their winning ways.

REAL-LIFE EXAMPLE:

Roger manages geographically dispersed teams, and he cannot be on site for all events or campaigns. When a success occurs in a particular region, Roger is quick to assign credit to the local team member by name. Even when he has played a role in that success, he reinforces the work done by the team member to ensure that he or she feels appreciated and to ensure that higher management is aware of his or her work. However, when less-than-desired outcomes arise, Roger usually assigns himself the blame by acknowledging he should have anticipated the problem and guided the local team member. "Usually" is the operative word as it is important for team members to maintain a sense of responsibility; they should not be shielded from negligent actions or lack of action.

TAKEAWAY:

Whether you are an individual contributor or a manager, ensure your team shares credit for successes, and if you are a manager, assume responsibility for losses.

#45
Leadership and Motivation

Which is more effective at motivating someone, the carrot or the stick? It is an age-old question. Performance may be stimulated by the promise of rewards or the fear of the consequences of failure. However, the operative word should be "and" not "or." Both incentives and deterrents, working together, are most effective.

People generally perform better over a longer period of time when they are positively motivated to perform as opposed to being scared of negative consequences. Psychologists have demonstrated this in countless experiments. A simple example is when you compare your reaction to two restaurant servers, one who says with obvious enthusiasm, "Welcome. May I take your order?" and another who says the same thing in a monotone voice. Your reaction to the first server, who seems more positive, would be to reciprocate the enthusiasm and to make an effort to be more polite in return.

Are you familiar with schools that do not issue traditional grades, yet almost every student still passes? In a class of overachievers, this grading system may work well, but this type of performance evaluation would not work in the corporate world because not everyone has the same level of motivation. With those who are selfish or self-centered, you, as the leader, must be willing to carry and use a big stick. Not only will you eliminate underperformers on your team, but also you will send a reinforcing message to those who remain on your team that underperformers will not be tolerated. At the same time, you should offer carrots (rewards) to those who exceed expectations. Others greatly appreciate and notice spot bonuses, extra time off, or other rewards of recognition.

REAL-LIFE EXAMPLE:

A good example of what is described above is a team of rowers or crew. Envision two boats that can accommodate ten rowers that are racing along a river. Boat A has ten people, but one rower is not rowing in unison with the other nine. Boat B has only nine synchronized rowers and one empty seat. Which boat will likely win? Easy ... boat B. Not only does it not have to put up with the drag of the poor rower in boat A, but also boat B has less "dead weight" to move through the water.

Why is boat A's rower out of sync? Can the situation be corrected, or can his or her performance be increased using different motivation? If not, then he or she should be dropped as a member of the team. Conversely, the rowers who do perform find their motivation in winning races, so it is clear they will work hard for the team.

TAKEAWAY:

When it comes to motivation, a combination of the carrot and stick is likely to be your best approach, as it will motivate many and rid your organization of those who are undeserving.

#46
Care about Your Team Members' Careers

Manage your team members' careers as if they were your own. Ask them what their aspirations are and where they see themselves a year or two down the road. Help find a way for them to get there—it will probably mean that they will become more efficient and effective under you.

If you have a manager who does not engage you in this manner, then be proactive yourself. Share with your manager your aspirations, and propose a way for you to achieve them over time. The most effective way to ensure his or her support is to demonstrate how your aspirations will benefit the organization or support its objectives. For example, if your manager is charged with creating $2 million in new accounts, tie that into your desire to be an account manager, and show how you can help him or her achieve this increase while helping yourself develop new skills. Oftentimes, those at higher levels in an organization have a better perspective of the talent pool, so raise your career aspirations with your manager's manager as well.

You probably spend more time at the office than at home—your team members are your family at the office. While one's work life should never supersede family life, care about the others you work with as if they were family. This does not mean learning all about their personal lives; it just means you should relate to them on a human level and understand that they are not automatons.

REAL-LIFE EXAMPLE:

Edwina had an employee who was new to the professional workforce and did not know what she wanted to do one year down the road. She had no career aspirations though she knew she wanted to succeed in a professional work environment. Edwina proposed they meet periodically to talk about things that interested the employee and find work projects that overlapped those interests. Taking the time to work with the employee helped the employee understand the areas in which she needed further development and also helped Edwina become a better manager.

TAKEAWAY:

Realizing one's career aspirations takes a little initiative and support from management. If you are an individual contributor, show how you want to grow. If you are a manager, take an interest in your team members' career goals and help them develop their potentials. Doing this not only makes the team stronger, but it also helps your team perform better.

#47
Managing Your Manager

Are you familiar with the phrase "managing your manager"? If not, then it may seem odd to you. It does not mean you should become a know-it-all or take a superior tone with your manager. It does mean, however, that you should be proactive in helping set your own objectives and tasks with your manager. A good manager will appreciate your self-starter attitude.

If your manager has promised his manager to deliver something, then help him or her to remember. If your manager has promised to deliver something to you, make sure you get a commitment as to when he or she will get it to you. If it is in a few days, remind him or her the day before. If your manager still does not get it to you, then suggest a way for you to help him or her.

There is a fine line between being a pest and being assertive. Use your best judgment and your manager's personality as guides as to how to best "manage your manager"—subtlety often works best. Remember, your job is to make your manager look good by helping him or her fulfill objectives. If reminding your manager of commitments helps him or her achieve objectives (which also are yours), then you are being a good employee.

REAL-LIFE EXAMPLE:

To support his annual objectives, Philip does his best to identify the goals that his team should pursue each quarter. He then circulates these to his manager, colleagues, and team members for their input. Waiting for his manager to come to him with the goals means that Philip would be passively supporting his manager. By demonstrating that he is a self-starter, Philip earns respect from his manager and frees up his manager's time to do other things.

Incidentally, Philip has team members who manage him by doing the above as well. It almost goes without saying, but these team members regularly garner the top ratings during the organization's annual review process.

TAKEAWAY:

Managing your manager may empower you to set your own agenda and earn his or her respect, *but* use common sense to ensure that your actions are not (mis)interpreted as coming from a self-promoting or disrespectful subordinate.

#48
Whistle-Blowing

Whistle-blowing is an issue of ethics and legality. It is difficult to be explicit about what you should report, but if you feel something is not quite right, then talk to your manager, your organization mentor (not an outside mentor), or the Human Resources Department.

Ensure your motives are clear. Is what you perceive to be a problem grounded in objective observation, or could you be motivated by other factors? Try to have some degree of proof before disclosing your suspicions. Telling someone that you suspect something without any facts to back your claim up may end up making you look bad. However, having facts to substantiate your claim will enhance your objective credibility.

In some jurisdictions and in all fair organizations, you will not be targeted because of your disclosure. Top companies even utilize third parties that will confidentially collect employee suspicions so that potential whistle-blowers can remain 100 percent anonymous. If you ever feel unfairly treated, you should consider seeking legal redress.

REAL-LIFE EXAMPLE:

Carol Anne worked for an organization in which some employees began to suspect that a finance employee was paying for personal expenses with organization resources (an infraction) and failing to reimburse the organization (embezzlement). The employees raised their suspicions with management after they had collected some facts to support their claim. A subsequent investigation uncovered possible embezzlement that was magnitudes greater than the whistle-blowers even suspected. The accused embezzler resigned in disgrace and was arrested for her suspected criminal behavior. Just as importantly, the organization changed its processes to prevent this from happening in the future. The whistle-blowers remained anonymous and were privately rewarded for their brave actions.

TAKEAWAY:

If you suspect unethical behavior in your organization and have some corroborating proof to support your suspicions, you should report your suspicions to the appropriate personnel. Respect the anonymity of whistle-blowers and ensure that any future whistle-blowers are not dissuaded from coming forward.

#49
Tooting Your Own Horn

You know you have done a good job, but how do you ensure your managers and colleagues know? Your manager likely does know, as managers are more aware of what is going on than you may realize. Colleagues are less likely to know of your achievements, as one would expect.

Let us say that you have done something remarkable and you want people to know. What is the best way of communicating your achievement without seeming like a braggart?

If you are asking this question, then you are starting from the right perspective. You should always be aware of how you come across to others. If you are worried about not seeming humble, then you probably are humble.

There are a number of ways to toot your own horn. One way is to mention your good news casually in a passing conversation or as a brief line in an email about other things or a weekly update. You should already be providing these updates to your manager and other interested parties to keep them informed of your progress toward your objectives, but this forum also gives you an opportunity to mention your good news. If you are a manager, you can acknowledge the success of one of your team members, which, in turn, is a success for you.

REAL-LIFE EXAMPLE:

An organization Mark worked for invested thousands of dollars so his team could recruit prospective channel partners at an event in New Orleans. At the conclusion of the event, the prospective channel partners were asked to vote on the team that had given the best presentation. Mark's team was honored with first place, even though there were dozens of teams competing—many of which worked for organizations that had magnitudes larger revenues and more brand recognition. Mark communicated his team's success back to his manager by highlighting the contributions that each team member made during the presentation. Had Mark not tooted his team's horn, no one back at headquarters would have known. As a result, each team member received recognition, and Mark gained additional trust and respect from his team.

TAKEAWAY:

Do not be afraid to toot your own horn. Assume that if you do not do it for yourself, no one else will.

#50
The Name of the Game

As organizations grow in size, it becomes increasingly difficult to remember all of your colleagues' names. Nevertheless, strive to learn each person's name, and use it when addressing or referring to the person. You will be telegraphing that you acknowledge and respect that person.

Name recall is particularly important in business meetings. When introduced to someone, repeat his or her name. Try to address the person by name during the meeting, and be sure to acknowledge him or her by name at the end of the meeting. People like to hear their own names spoken, so addressing a person by name is particularly useful to diffuse stressful moments or disagreements.

You can use various mind tricks to help with recall, so use the one that works best for you. Some people memorize names by associating a person with something that is easy to remember. For example, "The man on the far right is named Reginald like my brother, and he comes from Colorado where we have our R&D center." In a meeting where you are introduced to a number of people for the first time, you could place their business (name) cards in front of you according to where they are sitting. This is not as discrete, perhaps, as other methods, but if you have difficulty remembering names, it may be a good solution for you.

REAL-LIFE EXAMPLE:

To acclimate faster at a new workplace, Sheila got a floor plan of the office from the office manager and wrote in who sat where to help her remember. In the next general staff meeting, she was able to say hello to everyone by name. It was a simple trick, but it worked!

One organization that Sheila worked for had many remote offices, and colleagues rarely met one another in person, so she created an organizational chart for her department, with names, titles, contact info, and photos of everyone. People were shy at first about putting their photos on the chart, but it became standard policy. Putting a face with a name helps!

TAKEAWAY:

Make it a point to remember others' names as a mark of courtesy and respect.

#51
Following Can Lead to Success

All leaders have been or still are good followers in some capacity. Good followers are considered good because they know when and how to act on instructions. Sometimes managers are unable to explain the "why" behind their decisions, as they may be poor communicators or they may have confidential information. No matter the reason, if you can learn to follow your manager's directions, others will see you as a loyal employee, and you will be afforded more opportunities in the future.

A relationship between a manager and his or her employee is founded on trust. The manager trusts that the employee will do what is needed to help the manager achieve his or her objectives and do so by following the instruction, implied or implicit, of the manager. The employee trusts that the manager has the employee's best interests in mind and will lead the team to success.

As an individual contributor, you may learn from your manager different leadership techniques or, if he or she is a poor manager, how not to lead. Either way, being in a position of follower allows you to polish your listening and interpersonal communication skills. Even if you feel you have skills superior to those of your manager, use the time you have in your current position to become an even better follower. Once you fully appreciate how followers think, you will be a much better leader when the opportunity arises for you.

Remember, you make yourself look good when you make your manager look good—it is your job to help him or her accomplish goals. If your manager succeeds, then you also will likely succeed.

REAL-LIFE EXAMPLE:

In Max's career, there have been several instances in which he has been asked to provide data to his manager. By the nature of the requests, he could tell that it was more appropriate not to ask how the information was to be used. As it turns out, some of those instances were to support the purchase of another organization or to spin off a division of his organization. Knowing when to follow and delivering as requested helped make Max a discreet Clutch Hitter.

TAKEAWAY:

Being a good follower is a critical skill and will help prepare you to be a better leader.

#52
Intra-Office Dating—Dangerous Liaisons?

The office is one of the top places where people develop lasting relationships. This is not surprising given how much time colleagues spend together. It is also a convenient place to find people with similar interests, goals, or values. But in terms of using your workplace as a place to flirt or find potential dates, it could be damaging for your career.

Be wary of using your workplace as a dating den. Many relationships will fail. And when they fail, they can fail in a very public, embarrassing manner. Personal details that you assumed were shared in confidence may suddenly be public knowledge. This can include innocuous comments about your manager or colleagues, or even something as intimate as what goes on in the bedroom.

If you do form a relationship with someone in your workplace, it is best to keep it as low-key as possible. Depending upon the circumstances, some people may (in)correctly draw the conclusion that the relationship is affecting one or both parties' objectivity. Many organizations specifically prohibit relationships between direct reports for obvious reasons. Be prepared for one person to transfer to another position or even resign if the organization has any concern about real or perceived favoritism.

REAL-LIFE EXAMPLE:

Not too long ago, an ex-astronaut was preparing to go to trial for the alleged kidnapping, battery, and burglary of a rival lover of a former colleague. This example is extreme, but it shows that even people in exalted professions, such as astronauts, are susceptible to making bad decisions when it comes to romantic involvement with colleagues.

TAKEAWAY:

If you engage in an intra-office relationship, be discreet and aware that if the relationship should end poorly, anything you said or did may become public knowledge around the office and could possibly tarnish your professional reputation.

#53
Waste and Be Wasted

Organizations have long felt cheated by employees who use organization resources for personal gain, such as non-work related calls or photocopies. While organizations still fear monetary losses, an increasingly important concern is the lost productivity of employees (e.g., web surfing, instant messaging, etc.). Whether some level of personal activity on the job is acceptable depends on many factors.

Many organizations have employed technologies that make employees available outside of traditional business hours. For example, many organizations issue BlackBerry® devices, laptops, home email access, mobile phones, etc. If you work for a multinational organization, then you may be invited (i.e., expected) to participate in conference calls held at unusual hours. Given the transition to a virtual 24/7 job, many employees have the expectation that occasional personal endeavors undertaken during traditional business hours is fair.

If you work for an organization that requires your availability outside of traditional work hours and your organization does not explicitly prohibit employees from using corporate resources for personal use, then occasional use within reason should be acceptable. If you have questions about what is acceptable, you should approach your organization's human resources personnel for clarification on policy.

There are some notable exceptions to the above opinions. If you have a job in which you should not be using organization resources for personal use (e.g., a retail assistant) or your organization must archive communications under law (e.g., financial institutions or governmental organizations), then any personal use of your organization's resources may be unethical or illegal.

REAL-LIFE EXAMPLE:

Norbert once worked for an organization that necessitated a lot of work outside of regular office hours. Because of the overlap of work and personal life, if an employee needed to take a few hours off during office hours to conduct personal business, for example having one's car serviced, then no formal time off was required. Management understood that the employees were conscientious and would not hesitate to catch up on work once at home. On the other hand, using organization resources such as the printer for personal gain (e.g., to print school reports for one's children) would not have been appropriate.

TAKEAWAY:

If a reasonable person would conclude that your productivity exceeds expectations, your organization will probably turn the other way when it comes to occasional web surfing, emailing, instant messaging, or time off for an errand.

#54
Overtime or Waste of Time?

Does your organization promote a work-life balance for its employees, or is overtime expected for those who seek promotions? Does your organization expect that you will always be available? Have you noticed the same people staying late time and again? Does that make them superior employees or poor time managers?

As with so many things, it all depends on the situation. The ideal employee is one who works as hard and effectively as he or she can during work hours so that overtime is not needed. However, if an occasional situation calls for overtime, an employee should project a will-do, team attitude and make himself or herself available for overtime.

If you are an employee who frequently works overtime, you should take an honest assessment of yourself to determine what the true cause of your overtime is. Is there something that you could do differently, or is the organization truly the cause?

If your honest self-assessment leads you to believe that your overtime is due to peer pressure to stay late or the organizational culture, then you should try to alleviate it by having a discussion with your manager about one of four remedies:

1. Request additional compensation (that is, if you are not already receiving it) in the form of a promotion or bonus.
2. Request assistance in the form of more manpower (short- or long-term).
3. Request modification of processes so that work is not already backlogged by the time it reaches your desk.
4. Request a combination of two or more of the above.

Put your concerns in writing. After you discuss them with your manager, follow up with an email outlining your discussion and the proposed remedy.

REAL-LIFE EXAMPLE:

At Sean's organization, 50 percent of a quarter's sales orders come in the last month of the quarter. In fact, about 25 percent of the quarter's sales orders come in the final days of each quarter. This puts an enormous strain on the sales operations team to book and ship the orders, which often means they have to work overtime to get the work done. Clearly, the sales team could employ better time management to close orders earlier in the quarter and put less pressure on the sales operations team to work overtime.

TAKEAWAY:

Occasional overtime and a will-do attitude may be critical factors for promotion, but chronic overtime suggests a problem with management, processes, and/or your efficiency.

#55
Back Up or Pack Up

We have all experienced data loss. Some of us have written a report, forgotten to save the document, and then lost the entire file; others of us have composed an important email that suddenly disappeared; others of us have had computer crashes through which important files were lost. Every day, individuals and organizations needlessly suffer from a loss of data due to the following:

- disaster (e.g., fire, hurricane);
- accident (e.g., dropping laptop, spilling coffee on the keyboard, or hitting "Save" instead of "Save As");
- technology failure (e.g., media failure, system crash);
- theft.

Statistics suggest that organizations that suffer a significant data loss face a 50 percent chance of being out of business within the subsequent twelve months. Think back to when you lost that important file—now magnify it by thousands, and you will understand how a business can fail because of data loss.

Remember the earlier tip on keeping good records (see "#13: Set the Record Straight")? This includes you taking the additional step of protecting your personal, valuable records from loss due to disaster, accident, or theft. Make it a regular practice to back up your personal data to a portable drive, an Internet storage account, or via email. If your organization does not have a formal backup policy, then suggest that one be put in place. Be sure to clarify if your organization's backup policy includes individual users (versus servers), as 60 percent of an organization's data typically resides on individual users' computers. It is also advisable to ensure that if you initiate personal backups at work that you will not be in violation of security regulations or laws; this is particularly important for government employees.

REAL-LIFE EXAMPLE:

Hamid was working on a long-term writing project that went through many versions, updates, and changes. Because the project was important to him, he continually made layers of backups to a backup drive, a portable USB stick, and even via email (by emailing himself a copy so that a copy sat on the servers of his email provider). If something had happened to the current version of his project, he would have been able to revert to the last backup with little loss of data or time.

TAKEAWAY:

When it comes to your data, protect it and yourself by keeping backups. A current backup in a safe place will help you recover the files you may have lost and get back to work more quickly.

#56
Relations with Executives

Do you look forward to interacting with executives in your organization? It is smart to be cautious about making a bad impression, but do not avoid the opportunities should they arise. To be successful, you will need to be comfortable talking to and sharing ideas with all levels of management. If you have some weaknesses, work diligently at addressing them so that when you do have interactions you will be confident.

Interacting with executives can help your career in various ways. Many layers of managers may exist between you and your organization's executives. Without direct contact, the executives may not have any knowledge of your contributions. Another possibility is that you may find a mentor (see "#79: Mentors Are Meaningful"). Executives oftentimes enjoy helping younger employees the way someone once helped them. By working with a mentor, you may learn more about your organization's strategy from a perspective that you normally would not have. Furthermore, your interactions may position you for special projects. For example, if a cross-functional team is put together to find ways to raise employee morale, then the executive you impressed in the hallway last week may nominate you to participate.

It is important to be yourself. Executives, as people, may consciously or subconsciously judge you, and when they do, they will likely judge you against your peers, not against themselves. They may ask themselves, "Is our organization utilizing this employee's talents to the maximum potential?" or "Does this person have a great future with our organization?" You should be genuine when conversing with executives. Employees who continually lavish flattery on executives may come across as sycophants interested only in getting ahead and not in contributing to the success of the organization.

Whether or not you expect to interact with executives, make sure you are an expert in your area of responsibility. Know your numbers, have opinions on how your role or department can be improved, and know as much as possible about your organization in general. In this way, you will always be prepared and have confidence. You should not be surprised if an executive asks you specifics about your role, since they are keen to learn as much "unfiltered" information about their organization as possible.

REAL-LIFE EXAMPLE:

Rashad has had the privilege of interacting with executives at the organizations he has worked for, up to and including the CEOs. No matter the scenario, all of the instances allowed Rashad to learn more about the organizations he worked for and more about how executives manage their challenges (e.g., dealing with members of the media, rallying employee morale, and interacting with high-level customers). In return, Rashad demonstrated that he was an expert in his area of responsibility and aspired to grow into expanded roles.

TAKEAWAY:

The opportunity for executive interactions should be welcomed as long as you are expert in your area of responsibility, care about the objectives of the organization, and are yourself. You will likely be judged against your peers, so you need not be the smartest, most educated, or best dressed to make a positive impression.

#57
Competing Head to Head with Peers

Eventually, you will find yourself competing against others to get ahead, whether it is competing for a new job, a promotion, or Employee of the Month. You may encounter three types of competitors:

1. Type A - This person recognizes you as a competitor and feels that you must lose for him or her to win.
2. Type B - This person recognizes you as a competitor but does not feel that you must lose for him or her to win.
3. Type C - This person does not recognize you as a competitor, even though you are.

So how should you deal with these types of competitors? Sun Tzu made the famous observation, "Keep your friends close and your enemies closer." This may indeed be a good strategy for type A. This competitor seeks to undermine you in order to succeed. Even though he or she may try to demean you or talk badly of you to others, the best action is to take the high road. Not acknowledging the type A as a competitor to his or her face will have the effect of not providing validation to him or her. Moreover, you may compete more effectively without the type A realizing what a true threat you are and knowing that you are actively competing against him or her.

Types B and C are much less threatening. Type B is a gracious competitor—as you should be. He or she may still want to win as badly as anyone else does, but will win through his or her own actions, not by undermining your actions. Type B's attitude is that he or she will succeed if worthy—may the best man or woman win. Type C may not be a competitive person at heart. When you are up against a type C, you should continue to be a type B. In other words, acknowledge the competition, but focus on your own performance.

REAL-LIFE EXAMPLE:

In Duane's first professional job, he found that there was a nearly identical employee in terms of his degree, age, and job responsibilities. It was immediately obvious that the other employee saw Duane as his competitor (i.e., he was a type A). Duane addressed the situation in three ways. First, Duane reached out to his competitor to establish rapport by inviting him to lunch and sharing perceptions of their workplace. Second, Duane focused on excelling at his area of responsibility and by building rapport with their managers through extracurricular activities, including sports and committees. Lastly, Duane never openly acknowledged the competition. Without the other employee realizing it, Duane was actively responding to the competitive threat by being a type B. After a series of promotions in terms of responsibilities (including a relocation), Duane leveraged his experience to take on a much more enriching position at another organization.

TAKEAWAY:

Throughout your career, you will directly or indirectly compete with colleagues for recognition, responsibilities, or promotions, so take the high road and focus on your performance to maximize your opportunities for success.

#58
Jargon or Group-Speak

ROI. OEMs. NGOs. LTL. SMS. Cloud computing. Bottom-line it. One throat to choke. Status update.

People frequently use acronyms or phrases that everyone in the respective department, profession, or organization comprehends. Within the appropriate group, jargon or group-speak is acceptable and efficient. To an outsider, these abbreviations and phrases may be indecipherable or ostentatious.

Always spell out the acronyms or use general terms when communicating with someone outside the group. It is a basic courtesy and for their benefit so they can contribute their expertise without becoming disconnected from the flow of discussion. This disconnection may actually end up in group-think—when members of a group speak an exclusive way and then begin to think an exclusive way. This prohibits creativity or outsiders from becoming part of the group. This can become particularly damaging in an organization reliant on innovation.

Eliminating the use of jargon or acronyms makes communications more clear and prevents the development of groupthink. It also prevents misunderstandings from occurring that may otherwise result in unintended or negative consequences.

REAL-LIFE EXAMPLE:

The high-tech industry is notorious for its use of acronyms. High-tech companies incorporate jargon when communicating internally, with suppliers or partners, and with their target customers, the public-at-large. It is even common that people across different departments within the same organization use different jargon, and it is taken for granted that this is the right way to communicate. It is no wonder that the general public often lambasts high-tech companies for making their products complicated and difficult to use.

TAKEAWAY:

Use language that is appropriate for your audience, as communication is only possible when the audience receives and understands the intended message.

#59
Grooming for Success

If you had to hire someone and you had two candidates: candidate one, who shows up tidy and clean, and candidate two, who shows up with bed-head, bad breath, and looks unwashed, whom would you hire? All things being equal (e.g., qualifications), most people would choose the tidier person. The effort that candidate one made to look professional shows he or she respects you enough to look nice, has a better understanding of how the "real world" works, and probably has more control generally.

Grooming includes hairstyling, bathing, cleanliness, and tidiness of one's person. Some people might think it is silly to spend time on this topic, but you would be surprised at how easy it is to overlook the small things that make a big difference.

No one should care how much you spend on your grooming or where you shop or have your hair cut. As long as you are clean, look tidy, and do not have outrageous style, you will be appropriate for most workplaces.

REAL-LIFE EXAMPLE:

If you have seen the movie *Working Girl*, with Melanie Griffith, then you will remember her character's transformation from New Jersey secretary to Manhattan executive—she made just a few changes to her appearance, and voila! Colleagues began to take her seriously and she became a power player. Remember nothing substantive changed initially—it was her outward appearance that opened the door of opportunity.

TAKEAWAY:

Packaging yourself includes not only your skills and capabilities but also your outward appearance. Good grooming generally reinforces a person's confidence and makes the person more appealing.

#60
Dressing to Impress?

Although most people try to be egalitarian, how we look does play a role in how or what people think of us. In a professional environment especially, what you choose to wear is part of how you "sell" yourself to others. Those who pay attention to the details of their dress are often perceived to be more professional and effective.

Dressing for success does not mean wearing expensive clothing or breaking your budget to buy clothes you cannot afford. For most businesses, it means "value professional" attire, for which one pays a small premium for quality but not a huge premium for excess.

Dress appropriately for your workplace. If the culture is truly casual, at least wear clean and unwrinkled clothing. Remember, it is always better to be overdressed than underdressed. Avoid the following:

- overly casual clothing like shorts and t-shirts in an office environment where ties are common;
- torn, stained, or visibly wrinkled clothing;
- provocative clothing more appropriate for non-work socializing.

In the heyday of the dot-com era, the U.S. workforce underwent an interesting change as casual Fridays expanded to more organizations. Some went everyday casual. Others encouraged, or at least did not discourage, casual slacks and skirts. Not surprisingly, some people began to test the limits. It was not uncommon to see people in t-shirts or outfits more appropriate for clubbing. In some departments, people were allowed to wear almost anything as long as they got their work done. Shorts, untucked shirts, and sandals were acceptable at many organizations.

What happened when the dot-com bubble burst? One of the first things to change was people's attire. As organizations were forced to lay off employees, many came to the quick (re)realization that those who dress for success probably mean business and would add the most value to the organization.

REAL-LIFE EXAMPLE:

Carter had a colleague whom a customer lodged a complaint against for wearing provocative tops. She was in sales, and although some sexists may suggest that a woman can sell more by dressing provocatively, the customer was offended enough to ask that she either dress in a less revealing shirt or be removed from the account.

TAKEAWAY:

People judge you by the way you dress, especially when they are not privy to your actual work or are shallow. Most likely, they are subconsciously judging you and not even aware of it. Outrageous dress may send an incorrect signal or make others uncomfortable.

#61
Use Common Scents

After considering grooming and dress, one cannot fail to mention the importance of how one smells. After all, there is no point to looking well-groomed if one has body odor. Fancy clothes will not mask the smell of nervous perspiration or general uncleanliness.

Everyone should be able to address body odor by washing, using deodorant, and wearing clean clothes. If you have a perennial problem, then you may want to talk to your doctor. If you are a smoker, then there may not be much that you can do, unless you desire to address your addiction. In terms of odor prevention, men should consider wearing undershirts, as they keep one warm in the winter and dry in the summer.

If you are generally well-groomed but have a bad day, during which a colleague bumps into you with his caramel latte or it is particularly hot and humid, you want to be able to make yourself and others more comfortable by eliminating the bad smell. Try to have a plan B or plan C for office wardrobe malfunctions. Plan B may be to try to cover the smell by using an adequate (but sparing) amount of perfume or cologne. Plan C may be to keep an emergency shirt in your desk or car trunk. You are certainly not expected to have a complete backup wardrobe, but having emergency clothing available may make you more comfortable and confident.

REAL-LIFE EXAMPLE:

After receiving complaints from airline passengers in a gate area, a gate agent had to approach a passenger emitting foul odors and ask him to take a shower and change into fresh clothes before being able to board a flight. The airline provided the clothes and booked the passenger on the next flight, but can you imagine the passenger's embarrassment? A little self-awareness goes a long way.

TAKEAWAY:

A little common "scents" makes a positive impression.

#62
Breath of Life

Unpleasant breath would not be a topic if there were not problems with this in every workplace. It is common for unpleasant breath to develop over the course of the workday, which is not surprising. Following one's morning-ritual tooth brushing, people drink, eat, and possibly smoke—each an activity that may contribute to bad breath.

The fact is that when you have bad breath, people will notice. Their response may range from an unpleasant thought to outright avoidance. It is not only embarrassing for the person with the bad breath, but it is also uncomfortable for the person who may inevitably have to point out the issue.

Practice prevention of unintentional bad breath by avoiding activities that may contribute to it, or at least mask the odor by using breath mints or spray. If the issue is ongoing, it may be halitosis and something you may want to discuss with your doctor as tooth brushing alone will not solve the problem.

REAL-LIFE EXAMPLE:

Helmut is aware that through the course of some days his breath gets a little stale or his mouth a little dry. Therefore, he keeps an array of breath fresheners in his desk drawer. For quick refresher, he utilizes handy breath strips. After a spicy lunch, he tends to brush his teeth using a travel toothbrush and paste he got from a pharmacy's travel toiletries selection.

TAKEAWAY:

You will do yourself and those around you a favor if you brush your teeth after eating and ensure that your breath is fresh throughout the workday.

#63
Another Handy Tip

The need to wash your hands throughout the day, especially after a visit to the restroom, cannot be overemphasized. Amazingly, many people elect against washing their hands or substitute a cursory rinsing for actual washing. Rinsing one's hands is not effective at preventing germs from spreading.

Studies have shown that our hands pick up all sorts of germs from our environment (e.g., car steering wheel, subway handle, computer keyboard, shaking hands). If you carry these germs back to commonly-used items like your keyboard, phone, purse or laptop case, the germs may spread or lead to recontamination.

Do your colleagues and yourself a favor by practicing good hygiene—wash your hands with warm soap and water.

REAL-LIFE EXAMPLE:

Filene and a colleague concluded a meeting with a customer at the customer's place of business. As the three were leaving the conference room for the main entrance, Filene's colleague asked to stop in the men's room. Filene and the customer chatted in the hallway while waiting. As it turned out, this restroom was for a single user at a time and had a very thin door. Filene and the customer could not help but overhear Filene's colleague doing his business. Not three seconds after the toilet flushed, Filene's colleague emerged and put out his hand to shake goodbye to the customer. Filene could see the horror that swept across the woman's face. She reluctantly shook hands and went straight to the restroom (probably to wash her hands!).

TAKEAWAY:

Washing your hands is critical to preserving your health, the health of those around you, and maintaining a professional reputation.

#64
Handed Down for Generations—The Handshake

Anthropologists say that the handshake originated as proof that a person felt comfortable enough with another person's hygiene or health to shake his or her hand. Today, handshakes say more about how you feel about yourself. Does your handshake say you are confident? Nervous? Strong? Weak? Dominant? Timid?

A confident handshake at the beginning and ending of business interactions or during introductions is an opportunity to give people a positive opinion of you. When the situation calls for it, be forthcoming; do not hesitate to extend your hand first. Give a medium-strong handshake with one or two pumps, make eye contact, use the person's name, and move on. Do not try to dominate the handshake. Adjust your pressure according to the person with whom you are shaking hands.

Some unique situations call for modified behavior. If you are with your manager, allow him or her to extend his or her hand first. If you are in a meeting with several people of varying positions, then the standard is to shake hands in descending order of title. Some business cultures may frown upon a junior staff member offering his or her hand to a more senior staff member. If your particular organization is more traditional, then adapt to the norms and wait until the more senior individual has offered his or her hand to you.

There also are protocols for shaking hands in different cultures. If you are interacting with others from outside of North America, you would do best to look up the proper protocol. In Japan, bowing is traditionally used instead of a handshake. However, as the world shrinks, handshakes are becoming more commonplace, especially if the other person assumes that your inclination is to shake hands (i.e., if an American calls upon a Japanese person while visiting Japan).

What about wet hands? Keep a handkerchief in your pocket or in your purse to dry your hand discreetly if needed. When a nervous person with a wet hand shakes your hand, the most polite response is to ignore it. If you have an opportunity, wait a few seconds and then discretely dry your hand. The wet handshaker may feel better that you did not instantly try to shake off his or her handshake.

REAL-LIFE EXAMPLE:

Benjamin has interviewed nearly one hundred candidates for positions in his organizations. He has discovered that there is a strong correlation between a candidate's handshake and a candidate's overall interview performance. Those who had a light, uninspiring handshake often failed to demonstrate passion for their past positions and were not particularly convincing in their interest for the new opportunities. Those who had clammy hands exhibited nervousness, at least at the beginning of the interview. As you might expect, those who had firm, confident handshakes performed well during the interview.

TAKEAWAY:

Let your handshake introduce you—a firm but friendly grip will convey the type of person you are.

#65
Dressing Your Workspace for Success

Quick, who is more effective? The person with piles of papers and files burying his or her cube or the person who is so organized that there is nary a paper on the desk? One may be a workaholic who does not have time to organize his or her work area while the other may be a lazy person who obviously does not have enough to do.

The organization or disorganization of your desk is a strong indicator of the quality of your work and job performance. Likely, nine out of ten times, the organized person is organized in other areas like delivering tasks on time, presenting quality work, and being open to new challenges. The people with the piles of papers burying their desks are generally disorganized and more difficult to count on to deliver on time.

Of course, there are exceptions to this rule. But if you want to present an image of someone who is in control, organized, and effective, then keeping a tidy workspace is essential. It is easy. Remove unnecessary items from your work area; create a filing system that works for you; keep your drawers organized by using desk caddies; or ask colleagues with tidy workspaces how they keep their spaces organized.

REAL-LIFE EXAMPLE:

Early in Fred's career, he had two colleagues: one whose cubicle looked like it was ready for a magazine photo shoot and another whose cubicle looked like a tornado had blown through it. Over a period of time, through observation and interaction, Fred came to the opinion that the colleague with the organized cube was the overall better employee and had everything he aspired to in his personal life. The other colleague was habitually behind, frequently offered excuses, and always seemed to undergo dramas outside of the office. Offhand remarks from executives suggested that they, too, felt the organized employee was a greater contributor than the sloppy employee.

TAKEAWAY:

Maintain an organized workspace to make it easier for you to perform your duties. It will also show others that you are in control and effective.

PART II: TIPS FOR OUTSIDE THE OFFICE—HOW EXTRACURRICULAR ACTIVITIES CONTRIBUTE TO YOUR SUCCESS

How your colleagues see you has a lot to do with who you are outside the workplace. Some people remain one-dimensional to their colleagues because no one at the workplace gets to see who the person outside the office is. Your personal pursuits paint a vivid picture as to the type of person you are. When you hear that Javier is a regular at the gym, what impression do you have? How about when you hear that Kendra is a volunteer at the Red Cross? Most people would form positive impressions of both of these people. Certainly, you should be yourself and pursue what interests you, especially outside of the office. But be aware that others will draw conclusions about you when they learn of your extracurricular pursuits, whether their assessments are fair or not.

#66
Excellent—You're Already Reading

Are you familiar with the expression "well-read"? It is an important part of being well-rounded. Regular readers tend to gain a broader perspective of life. Try to read a respectable daily newspaper and one book per month, if not more. The combination of these two reading habits will keep you informed about a wide range of topics. In fact, the newspaper alone should have a tremendous impact on your knowledge. For example, you will know what is happening in international relations, politics, local news, business (especially important), sports, entertainment, and even details of local promotions (i.e., potential competitive information).

When it comes to books, there are few poor choices. Read for fun as it may improve your mental well-being. However, at least twice a year you should read a book that is related to your field of expertise or general business. For example, if you are a manager (certainly an aspiring manager), read a popular book on management. If you do not know where to start, buy a bestseller from an online store, or ask your local bookstore for recommendations. Most large chains have shelves with bestsellers or staff picks.

Maintain a list of books that you have read or plan to read. Did you participate in a summer reading program at your library when you were younger? Do you remember how satisfying it was to add another book to the list and get closer to earning the certificate for free fries from McDonald's? Seeing a list of what you have read can provide a very satisfying feeling, especially as the list gets longer and more diverse. Try to pick out one good idea or takeaway from each book that you can implement in your life—there are a lot to choose from in this book! Keeping track of the books you read makes it easier to recall where you learned something interesting and serves as a reminder of what you have already read.

Weave into your conversations a concept or anecdote from one of your books or the daily news, and you will most likely make a positive impression on those with whom you are conversing. You will come across as well-rounded and informed, giving your statements or arguments more weight and gravitas.

REAL-LIFE EXAMPLE:

Noelle is an avid reader but only recently started keeping track of the books she reads. She regularly reads two to three books per month and has been doing so for years. After having read so many books, she cannot keep track of where she remembers reading what or if she even really liked a certain book. Now she keeps a list in Excel, including title, author, genre, and a brief synopsis and review of the book. If there are any particular quotes she wants to remember, she makes note of them as well.

TAKEAWAY:

Reading is an investment you make in yourself, whether your reading is for fun or for broadening your knowledge of current events and business acumen. No one who is well-read can ever be accused of being narrow-minded or shortsighted.

#67
Volunteerism Is Valuable

Volunteering for a greater cause is a wonderful thing to do because your actions may help others. This tip would end here if volunteerism were 100 percent altruistic. Say that you already volunteer or plan to volunteer outside of the office. How might your generosity toward a greater cause improve your standing in the workplace? Put simply, others may learn of your volunteerism and will respect you for it. Some workplaces even organize volunteer activities, provide incentives to volunteer, or offer time off. Investigate your organization's policies to determine if anything overlaps with your interests.

Not everyone shares the same concern for specific causes. That is one reason why there are so many causes in existence. Keep in mind that even if you think a cause is important, others in your office may not appreciate being put in a position where they feel they have to support you. For example, if you post an invitation in the break room to join you in planting trees, you are passively promoting your cause but not making others feel bad. If, however, you ask your colleagues to sponsor you in a 10K run that will raise funds for a new athletic gym, you are aggressively asking them to support your cause and not making it easy for them to decline. People should always feel good about supporting causes—it is a sure way for people to remain supportive and passionate.

What about selling goods and services on behalf of your children, nephews, or nieces? Of course, you want to help children go to camp, but many people will find you annoying if you put pressure on them to buy cookies, candies, discount books, etc. And your colleagues may, out of false guilt, feel compelled to buy. If you are going to target your workplace, then check with your office manager or Human Resources Department if you can post a voluntary sign-up sheet. Those who really want the Thin Mints or David's Cookie Dough will sign up willingly.

REAL-LIFE EXAMPLE:

During the course of recruiting new employees, Felix has found that those who list volunteer work tend to be better liked by the hiring teams than those who did not list any volunteer work. One prospective employee even used her time between jobs to volunteer for an earthquake relief organization, using some of her career skills and learning new ones. Her volunteer efforts outweighed a light résumé and allowed her to be hired to the position she coveted.

TAKEAWAY:

Being a compassionate human being is more important than being a success, but if you volunteer outside the office, it may help your professional standing. There are many ways to volunteer, so do what works within your schedule and speaks to your heart.

#68
Expertise in Non-Related Fields Is Truly Relative

A valuable way to broaden your skills set is to develop expertise in a field totally unrelated to your day job. Having varied interests helps to round you out as a person, makes you more interesting, and makes your life more enjoyable. As you develop expertise in your particular career, you may complement that by also becoming more expert in your favorite hobby or something totally new to you.

Diversifying your areas of expertise will not only help you gain a different perspective, but also your range and depth of experience and knowledge may impress others, especially those with whom you work. Life is more than just about work. After all, we work in order to live and not the other way around. Enjoying one's career is certainly desirable but not always possible. Sometimes we end up working in jobs we never expected. Therefore, developing skills in other areas may help fill an unfulfilled area of interest for you and help you gain knowledge that may help advance your career or possibly help you move in a new career direction, if you desire.

Most importantly, as you advance in your career, you may find the stress also increases with each job advance. As such, it is helpful to have an outlet outside of work that allows you to focus on something that is unrelated to your day-to-day work stresses. Learning is a lifelong process. As you find enjoyment in learning new things in areas that interest you, you also will become more interesting to others and become more well-rounded as a person.

REAL-LIFE EXAMPLE:

Marlena is known as a professional media consultant. However, when she was younger, she aspired to work for the Foreign Service. Immediately after obtaining her undergraduate degree, she passed the examination and completed the interview process. Although her career path went another direction, she still has a deep interest in international relations. Just passing the exam is considered difficult, so when colleagues learn of Marlena's past accomplishment and current interests, they are often impressed and think of Marlena in a different light. Because her background is unique, colleagues also remember it and approach Marlena for her insights when relevant topics arise.

TAKEAWAY:

Developing expertise in fields unrelated to your career can be personally enriching and professionally rewarding.

#69
Personal Fitness Suggests Work Fitness

Who would not agree that keeping in shape is desirable for your health? It is also good for your career. How? Exercise will keep your mind sharp and build your stamina. But beyond the intrinsic values, it is important to know that your colleagues form judgments about you based on your physical fitness.

If you are a very in-shape person, many people will respect you for that, if not envy you. They will assume that your self-control in the gym or on the court will carry over into the conference room. This may seem superficial, but most people form judgments subconsciously. Acknowledging this reality can help you if you choose.

For example, a former colleague formed instant perceptions of others based on their physical fitness. The colleague considered an out-of-shape person as one who lacked self-control and, therefore, not capable enough to advance in his or her career.

REAL-LIFE EXAMPLE:

Carmen has known numerous colleagues who were in tip-top shape and who always found time to get in a workout, whether they were at home or on the road. They did not boast of their exercise regimens, but envious colleagues and even customers often asked them about the regimens. Most people commented that they wished they had the will to exercise. It may come as no surprise that the tip-top shape employees were also stars within their organization.

TAKEAWAY:

Aside from the health benefits of being physically fit, know that being in shape will improve others' perceptions of you and being out of shape will hurt others' perceptions of you.

#70
There Is an "I" in Team Sports

Team sports are an enjoyable way to be physically fit, have fun, learn a team approach, and network in a less formal environment (especially if you are good at your chosen sport!). If your organization sponsors a team sport or if colleagues have organized a team outside of the office—such as bowling, softball, cricket, or golf—then consider joining. If you are very motivated, then volunteer to establish and/or manage the organization's team. Your willingness to lead and manage will show your colleagues that you have leadership skills that may easily be adapted from the field to the office.

Honesty in the workplace is crucial, but it is also critical in sports. Sportsmanship envelopes many ideals of on-field behavior, and honesty is one critical ideal. For as much as sports can help elevate your profile in your organization, poor sportsmanship, especially dishonesty, can harm your reputation just as quickly. When playing with colleagues, be generous. For example, if you are in a tennis match with a colleague and he or she hits a ball close to the line, be generous and call it in. Otherwise, he or she could, rightly or wrongly, think (and "think" is the operative word) that you cheated him or her, and tell others. You would end up losing more than just a point.

Good sportsmanship is also about making the game an enjoyable experience for others, so do your best to control your temper. Sometimes people mask embarrassment or frustration with a verbal admonition to oneself. Others may interpret your frustration as anger and think of you as quick-tempered. Using colorful language also comes across as undignified and unprofessional. If you strike out or let a pop fly get past you, then use humor to diffuse your embarrassment. Remember it is absolutely taboo to criticize others for a similar mistake. Good sportsmanship with colleagues is as much about establishing your image, if not more, than the outcome of the game or match.

REAL-LIFE EXAMPLE:

Tristan has always enjoyed his workplace's team sports experiences. He always keeps in mind that sports are a way to build bridges and reinforce his reputation. In tennis, he is generous with calling his opponents' balls in. In golf, he never takes "gimmes" and always putts out. He also has voluntarily managed several office golf tournaments that drew senior executives and customers. It made a positive impression when Tristan, as a lower-level employee, oversaw the well-run tournaments and presented winners with trophies (especially when the winners were executives).

TAKEAWAY:

Round out your image by engaging in extra-office sports with colleagues. You may not be a superstar in the office yet, but on the field, even a novice player who takes initiative and practices good sportsmanship demonstrates skills that will translate well back in the office.

#71
Spouses Can Help You Sink or Swim

Popular media have long portrayed the influence, good or bad, that spouses or significant others may have on an employee's career. A recurring theme of the television show *Bewitched* was the interaction of the husband's manager with the husband's entire family. The wife seemed to play as big of a role in her husband's career as the husband himself.

Spouses or significant others typically play a minor role in how you perform at work, other than the moral support you receive, but your spouse or significant other can both help you and hurt you through the Halo Effect. That is, your colleagues form opinions of you based on not only your work performance but also on your entire person, including whatever is known of your personal life. For example, if your spouse has an impressive background or career, then it will reinforce others' perception of you as talented since like attracts like. It also suggests that you made a good decision in choosing your significant other. Conversely, if your spouse is perceived negatively, then your image may be tarnished.

The best policy is for spouses to remain disassociated from your work. After all, your organization should be judging you for your ability to achieve the objectives given to you. If a spouse does interact (e.g., organization picnic to which families are welcome) it is best for him or her to say nothing about what he or she knows about the business (even though you may be each other's confidantes when it comes to discussing your respective work). For example, it would be in poor taste for your spouse to say to a colleague, especially a manager, "It's too bad Teresa's division won't get its bonus because the sales team failed to meet its quota." As accurate as your spouse may be, it would be better to say nothing at all rather than show a comprehension of the organization's internal workings.

It is not uncommon for colleagues and their spouses to get to know each other socially. The rapport that is established may strengthen work relationships as colleagues can become more like friends, gaining trust and sharing information. But be careful what organizational information is shared. For example, information a spouse blurts out about an upcoming, yet unannounced, layoff may be interesting, but it does not show discretion. As noted earlier, gossip is for goners, so if you must, be on the receiving end, and ensure that you are never on the speaking end.

REAL-LIFE EXAMPLE:

Rob and Jessica have had the fortune of meeting many colleagues' spouses outside of their respective work environments. At a holiday party, a spouse of Rob's colleague had a little too much to drink and shared some indiscreet information her husband had shared with her about some other colleagues. After the party, the colleague's wife became the subject of jokes, and the colleague was no longer trusted with confidential information.

TAKEAWAY:

Try to keep your business and personal lives separate, but when they do overlap, be discreet about what is organizationally confidential.

#72
Industry Associations Yield Good Relations

Joining industry associations is an easy way to build networks, become certified, and keep abreast of developments in your career or industry area. If you are not already familiar with an association suitable for you, do not assume one does not exist. There are literally thousands of professional and industry organizations around the world. By interacting with others in your field, you will help yourself in three important ways:

1. You will learn from your peers who will help you perform better in your job.
2. You will develop a network that might help you land a better job in the future.
3. Your organization (particularly your manager) will respect you for actively participating in an association that can help you improve in your job.

Other benefits of joining associations include adding the membership as a note in your résumé, earning certification(s), or getting access to information not publicly available. Some jobs require certification, so joining an association may be obligatory to get that certification. Make use of whatever resources are available through that association to improve yourself, broaden your skills set, and learn of new opportunities.

REAL-LIFE EXAMPLE:

Ralph is a member of an IT professionals peer network. Although less formal than an industry association, the group meetings that take place among local members allow Ralph to interact and learn with a group of people he may not, under other circumstances, have met. They share issues and concerns they face professionally and talk about what has worked for each other. If the other members appreciate Ralph's contributions, he may have a good source of future job leads, should he ever need them.

TAKEAWAY:

Joining industry associations will help you excel in your current role and may even serve as the source of a future career opportunity with another organization.

PART III: TIPS TO MAXIMIZE YOUR JOB SECURITY

This section is devoted to helping you maximize your job security. Many factors beyond your control can adversely affect your job security, such as being acquired by another organization, downsizing, business cycles, or management changes. However, there are actions that you can take to better position yourself for job retention when cuts are inevitable.

#73
Degrees and Certifications

It is commonplace for companies to offer a subsidy for additional education as a benefit to employees and to ensure employees are skilled or knowledgeable. Unfortunately, many employees fail to take advantage of this excellent opportunity. The value of the benefit can range quite substantially. It may be limited to internal, during work hours, skills enhancement training, or it may include partial reimbursement for certification training. It may even include partial or total reimbursement for an MBA program, paid time off to pursue your degree, or coursework at Oxford University with business class airfare!

You should seriously consider taking advantage of your organization's education benefits. Not only will your internal worth increase as your performance increases, but you also will be more marketable outside your organization. Many organizations require that any coursework be germane to your job. Work with you manager to ensure both the organization's and your needs are met. Some general degrees or certifications to consider are:

- Bachelor or Master degree (especially an MBA)
- Certifications (e.g., CPA for finance people, MCSE for IT people)
- Presentation skills training
- Writing skills training
- Management skills training
- Sales skills training
- Time management skills training
- Foreign language skills training

If you feel you just do not have the time because of workload and family commitments, remember you must decide for yourself how much time and money you are willing to sacrifice, given the benefits you would gain. If you are serious about your success, you will find that the sacrifices of time, effort, and money are worthwhile. In fact, you may want to consider any sacrifices you make as investments in yourself.

REAL-LIFE EXAMPLE:

Jasmine's organization encouraged employees to pursue advanced degrees as long as they directly related to a person's job. Jasmine received a partial education reimbursement that she used toward an MBA at a private university. Jasmine would have pursued the advanced degree even without the partial reimbursement from her organization, but the benefit certainly helped!

TAKEAWAY:

Take full advantage of your organization's education benefits. You will become more valuable within and outside of your organization, as the knowledge you gain will not only help you in your current role, but it will also help accelerate you to the next stage of your career.

#74

Not a Foreign Idea:
Expat Assignments Pay Big Dividends

Is a foreign assignment a privilege or an inconvenience? The answer depends on many factors, but the biggest factor is you. For many employees, a foreign or expatriate (commonly referred to as expat) assignment is like walking up a moving escalator compared to walking up standard stairs. That is, it is a faster, fast track. An expat assignment may vastly broaden your knowledge and experience while bringing you a degree of prestige.

Some jobs may more easily translate into an expatriate posting. For example, an organization that has no international offices will likely not have expatriate positions available. If you are in an organization that already has expatriates serving, then you will increase your chances for consideration if you make it known that you are interested. A good organization plans its expatriate postings months, even years, in advance. Oftentimes, a new opportunity opens up only when a current expatriate chooses to return to his or her home country. By volunteering for an assignment, you may be considered as opportunities develop.

Some people are more inclined to enjoy an expat assignment than others. Research has shown that when expat assignments fail, they fail within the first year and are commonly due to family issues rather than work issues. Typically, the employee is so busy and challenged that he or she does not experience the same setbacks as the family. Sometimes the office can seem like a surrogate family, whereas the family at home has to establish a new network of friends and activities. Many books specifically cover expat assignments, so be prepared for what an assignment requires by doing research or talking to your manager or human resources.

REAL-LIFE EXAMPLE:

Johann and his family are in their third year of an expatriate assignment in the Middle East that has been far more rewarding than they envisioned. Although they have made sacrifices, such as being far from family and having to adjust to culture shock, the rewards have been greater. From a professional standpoint, Johann is involved with a significantly broader range of business challenges than he would have been in a domestic role. From a personal standpoint, he and his family have learned more about other cultures through extensive travel within the region while also learning more about their own culture through the eyes of other people. The experiences and knowledge they have accumulated have changed their lives forever.

TAKEAWAY:

An expat assignment can be highly rewarding, but it is critical that you are aware of the unique challenges you will face, professionally and personally, before you volunteer and move your family overseas.

#75
Mind the Bottom Line

Enhance your job security and increase your value by constantly thinking about ways to cut costs or increase revenues. In other words, challenge yourself to identify ways to increase profitability. If you work for a nonprofit, then focus on efficiency. While most organizations use a number of matrices to determine the current and future value of their business, profitability is the most important, hence the label, "the bottom line."

You may think that there are not many opportunities to cut costs or increase revenues in your area of responsibility. However, you may actually discover numerous opportunities if you think objectively. It is very easy to stop thinking about things with a fresh perspective, but challenge yourself to do so. Inefficiencies and untapped opportunities exist in every organization; a creative mind can come up with numerous suggestions. Your ideas do not have to be momentous or huge, as even simple ideas may yield savings. It is about real money—money that your organization can save or spend in better ways.

You may even identify savings outside of your area of responsibility. For example, in a large organization, it is typically the Facilities Department that oversees the lighting of an office. A facilities manager may set lights to automatically turn on at 6:00 a.m. and turn off at 10:00 p.m. to ensure that lights are on when people *may* be in the office. However, you may notice that almost no one arrives before 7:00 a.m. or stays past 7:00 p.m. Why should the lights automatically be on outside of those hours? Suggesting a change to the lighting schedule could save the organization substantial money and make the organization more environmentally friendly.

How about ways to increase your organization's revenues? Just because something is not already being done does not mean it could not or should not be done. Imagine that you are in the import/export group and you start to notice orders from China. As an informed employee, you know that your organization does not have a presence in China and may be foregoing substantial revenue potential. You might simply ask at the next employee meeting or through informal communications with your management contacts if the organization has done a formal study of entering the China market. You will demonstrate that you understand the true objectives of your organization (profitability), even though you may not directly be tasked with finding new sources of revenue.

REAL-LIFE EXAMPLE:

Isaiah noticed that in one country, his organization used different agencies to book travel because not everyone worked in the same office. His recommendation to pool travel bookings through a single travel agency helped save employees time booking travel and resulted in reduced agency fees.

TAKEAWAY:

Apply the concern you show for your personal budget to the spending and revenues of your organization. Any money you save or earn may be spent in better ways, for example, covering the pay raise you have been expecting.

#76
Volunteering for Additional Assignments

Volunteering for new assignments or special projects within your organization is a good way to promote yourself and enhance your value. When you volunteer for new assignments, you signal that you are a team player, willing to accept new challenges, able to take on additional work, and able to provide even more value to your organization.

Before you volunteer, ensure that you have your manager's permission and are caught up (or at least reasonably so) with your regular job duties. Taking on additional work without your manager's knowledge may lead to conflicts, perhaps because something you see as important is not important to your manager. Taking on additional work when you are already behind will not only make it more difficult for you to catch up, but it also will show people that you are unable to finish tasks to which you commit.

You can volunteer for many activities. Your manager likely has some responsibilities that he or she may be able to share with you. There may be some work your manager has with which you can assist. By freeing up your manager's time, you will help him or her focus on more strategic goals. Alternatively, most organizations have cross-functional teams that tackle specific short-term challenges. For example, many organizations have an efficiency team that is tasked with looking for ways to cut needless expenses across departments. Keep in mind that teams that have executive sponsorship have a higher profile and may help increase your name recognition among the executive staff.

Inform your manager that you want to continue to add value while growing your skills set and are looking for new ways to contribute. Your manager should realize that your initiative makes you a valuable employee, and he or she will gladly give you new assignments or find a cross-functional team in which you may fit.

REAL-LIFE EXAMPLE:

Chris' organization selected a small group of high performing employees from across the organization and split them into two teams named Blue and Red. Each team analyzed the current strategic direction of the organization and recommended changes. At the conclusion of the first phase, each team made separate presentations to the executive staff. After the executive staff heard the independent assessments, they took the best ideas from each team and formed a new team (aptly called Purple). The Purple team went on to do more thorough planning on behalf of the executive staff, and the executive staff recognized each team member for his or her participation.

TAKEAWAY:

Whether your goal is to increase your job security or be on the fast track to promotion, consider volunteering for additional work or intra-organizational activities.

#77
Great Idea: Suggestion Programs

Suggesting ways to cut costs and increase revenues is often communicated through an organization's employee suggestion program, but these programs can be useful for other things. Perhaps you believe that employees could benefit from presentation skills training, or the cafeteria would be more popular if a low-carb offering was added each day, or a softball team should be formed.

Employee suggestion programs can be personally rewarding for you for three reasons:

1. Your ideas may get the attention of the leaders of your organization, who likely will appreciate you thinking of ways the organization can improve.
2. Your ideas may be acted upon.
3. You may be compensated for your ideas!

As with most things, there is a fine line, which, when crossed, may make one's (presumably) good intentions be received negatively. Be mindful not to be a gadfly, someone who has numerous opinions about minor matters. If you use the employee suggestion program as a way to make obviously irrelevant suggestions (e.g., "Change the brand of paper clips because the other brand feels smoother."), you may be worse off than having not suggested anything at all.

What if your organization does not have an employee suggestion program? Aha! There is your first idea! Suggest it in a constructive manner and volunteer to assist with its creation (probably along with human resources, depending upon the size of your organization).

REAL-LIFE EXAMPLE:

Many years ago, Lillian used the "I Have an Idea" program at her then workplace to suggest the organization reduce communication costs by adopting the emerging technology of email instead of faxes. Ironically, the organization dismissed the idea at the time but rewarded Lillian with a gift certificate for her input. Of course, not long after, email became the standard within her organization and is now a major method of communication.

TAKEAWAY:

Intelligently applied, your organization's employee suggestion program can be a great way to add value to your organization, increase your value, and potentially benefit your pocketbook.

#78
Stay Close to the Money

Have you ever heard people say you should "stay close to the money"? It means the more directly your individual contribution fulfills your organization's mission, the more secure your job will be.

Assume you work for a nonprofit organization that provides hot meals for the hungry. If you work in the legal department, you may have a valuable role to play. But ask yourself this: "Is the organization's primary mission to file court documents?" No, the organization's primary mission is to feed people. Those who most directly work toward fulfilling that mission have more valuable roles. In this example, if expenses need to be cut, it is more likely that back-office employees would be cut before those who are on the front line, sourcing food to feed the hungry.

Consider your annual performance review. If you are able to show how you brought in revenue or saved a significant amount of money, you show your value to the organization through numbers. Numbers always work better than words, as they speak for you. When you stay close to the money, do not only what you can to generate revenue or decrease spending, but also quantify your contributions to the organization as much as possible. No one will be able to dispute your contributions, and it will be easier to press for the raise or promotion you seek.

In a for-profit organization, you may assume that salespeople are closest to the money and that their jobs are the safest. This is true if they perform. Underwhelming results are obvious, and underperformers are likely to lose their jobs. Consider an organization that has a partnership with another, where the first provides royalties to the second. As long as the first organization is pleased, the relationship manager for the second organization will continue to bring in revenue and enjoy job security.

REAL-LIFE EXAMPLE:

Holly was responsible for managing several product lines that generated a significant amount of revenue. Holly faced a predicament when one of her product lines was given to another employee to manage, and she was given more strategic, although non-revenue-generating, responsibilities. This was a double-edged sword for Holly. On the one side, a revenue stream was taken from Holly's oversight, which meant she might not have as much coverage of risk should her other product lines not perform well. On the other side, she was given more strategic responsibilities and more exposure to executives.

TAKEAWAY:

Stay close to the money—the more easily identifiable your contribution is to accomplishing your organization's mission, the stronger your job security.

#79
Mentors Are Meaningful

Mentors can teach you valuable lessons that are useful within your organization, to your career, and for life in general. Mentors may help you navigate political waters, develop your soft skills, provide career guidance, challenge your business acumen, or share a wide range of beneficial advice.

Seek out a mentor in your organization for greater job security. Alternatively, find a mentor outside your organization. Some lucky people actually have mentors who seek them out. Most of us, however, need to find one on our own. You will likely gravitate toward someone who has skills you wish to possess, has the confidence you seek to emulate, or has the career you hope to have one day. Mentors usually benefit from your fresh perspective or may just be naturally helpful people. Find someone you like and trust, but above all, find someone you respect.

Whatever the attraction, developing a relationship with one or several mentors over the course of your career will benefit you in countless ways. Mentors are typically more senior to you or have more experience—the best mentors will be a couple levels or more above you, as people at or just above your level will not be able to provide guidance in long-term growth. However, peer mentors prove valuable in some instances. Some mentors you will have for life, and others may be short-term. Not only will their advice help you expand and polish your skills set, but also the relationship that you build could insulate you when times are difficult, as your mentor may have a direct link to those who must make stay and cut decisions.

REAL-LIFE EXAMPLE:

Sebastian has had both formal and informal mentors. One organization for which he worked had a special talent program for rising stars that assigned mentors to young managers. Sebastian was assigned to a mentor outside of his area of expertise and was able to learn more about how the organization operated in ways he had never been exposed. Sebastian also has enjoyed learning from informal mentors, people whom he respected who have offered their advice and shared their knowledge. All Sebastian's mentors have helped him to grow professionally and develop confidence in his abilities.

TAKEAWAY:

Find a mentor either within or outside your organization. The advice and counsel this person may provide will help you grow in the present and possibly assist you in the future.

#80
What Have You Done for Us Lately?

"What have you done for us lately?" Assume your organization asks you this question each and every day. Your challenge is to answer the question convincingly. As much as you may have contributed to your organization's past successes, you need to be able to continually point to new contributions as a way of securing your future. If you are unable to convince people that you are worth keeping on the payroll, then your tenure at your organization will likely be short.

There is no better example of continually proving your value than when a person starts his or her own organization, turns it into a great success, sells public shares, and then is fired by the very board of directors whom he or she helped elect! If the founder of an organization can be fired, then imagine how Kyle, the sales superstar for five years running, can be let go for recent lackluster performance.

You can point to your past accomplishments to justify higher pay, but you are paid for what you will deliver in the future and not for what you have already delivered. Think of it this way: your past performance is a predictor of future performance. Maximize your job security by doing everything possible to deliver more value to your organization week after week, quarter after quarter, and year after year.

REAL-LIFE EXAMPLE:

Ryan has been in many organizations over the years. He has observed numerous instances in which a normally good contributor was eventually let go for declining performance. Usually, strong performers lose motivation for a variety of reasons, such as personal issues, dismay about management, inadequate pay, lost confidence in product offering, etc. Ryan observed that declining performance seemed to occur most commonly with salespeople who burned out or across all departments after mergers or acquisitions. In the former instance, it is easy to measure a salesperson's performance. In the latter instance, the new managers sometimes did not have an appreciation for employees' past contributions.

TAKEAWAY:

Because people are paid on future, not past, performance, continually demonstrate your value to your organization rather than relying on past successes to improve your chances for promotion and insulate you when times get tough.

#81
Don't Be Lost in Translation—
Turn Your Contributions Into Promotions

Does your organization recognize your value-add in terms of responsibility, public recognition, promotion, or compensation? If you believe the answer is "not enough," then there are things that you can do to increase the recognition.

Salespeople say that if one wants to get the order, then one has to ask for it. The same is true for recognition of your work. It is rare for organizations to proactively foster or reward most employees—even though most are hardworking and add value. Even worse, some organizations do not even proactively look after their star employees. Organizations may not realize how dissatisfied an employee is until the employee asserts himself or herself. So how do you toot your own horn?

Consider where you currently are in your career and where you would like to be in a specific amount of time. If after an honest self-assessment you think you are worth more to the organization than for what you are being recognized, then you should proactively develop a plan with your manager, his or her manager, and/or the Human Resources Department. Make sure you suggest what you want because no one can read your mind.

Employees often ask how to go about getting a promotion. Much depends upon the organization, the manager, the position, and the employee. Have an objective conversation that politely reminds the organization of your contributions (especially if you are steadily increasing them) and your goals. If you are a rising star, your message will likely be received with appreciation and fear. The appreciation will come from the plain reality that you are important to the success of the organization; the fear will come from the plain reality that if the organization does not provide what you feel you are worth in the marketplace, you are likely to seek employment elsewhere.

Replacing employees, especially star performers, is expensive. The organization will not just lose your contributions, but it may have to replace you with a lower performing person at a higher salary and possibly even at the cost of paying recruitment firm fees. Usually, increasing an employee's compensation will be a lower cost than hiring and training a new person.

REAL-LIFE EXAMPLE:

Damien has always made sure to discuss his long-term goals with whomever his manager was at the time. By proactively discussing his goals and making his managers aware of his plans, his managers are able to look out for related opportunities for him. This has led to several promotions and special, high-visibility assignments.

TAKEAWAY:

Employment is a matter of supply and demand. If you put yourself in high demand through consistent, identifiable contributions to your organization, and you respectfully communicate to your organization what your expectations are, then you increase your likelihood of being rewarded.

#82

When the Going Gets Tough, the Tough Get Protective

All organizations run into difficult times. A downturn can be due to regular business cycles, a general malaise in the economy, or a natural disaster, but the result is usually a cost-cutting initiative aimed at protecting the organization's bottom line. The cost cutting may be surgically precise or may be a shotgun approach, such as having each department cut 10 percent.

If you are implementing some of the advice in this book and are finding new ways each day to increase your value to your organization, then you likely will be well positioned within your organization to weather tough times. Nevertheless, when tough times are foreseeable (e.g., economic recession, general sales decline, etc.) put your value-add to your organization into higher gear.

Without being a braggart, ensure that your manager and *his or her manager* recognizes your value-add. His or her manager should be included because oftentimes it is middle management that bears the brunt of downsizing. It is possible that your manager is unable to communicate his or her own contributions successfully, so you should ensure that your contributions are not overlooked. There are instances of middle management being terminated, while the lower level staff are retained and eventually promoted in responsibilities, title, or salary. This promotion through attrition is common, so ensure you are well positioned in case this unfortunate opportunity presents itself.

REAL-LIFE EXAMPLE:

Ariel experienced a lot of turnover in the levels above her and was unsure whether her new managers would recognize her contributions. She knew she would have to prove herself to her new managers over time, and she did not want to delay in demonstrating her abilities and contributions. She decided to send weekly updates to whomever her manager was at the time and list her objectives for the week and the progress she made. In this way, her manager would know exactly what Ariel was doing and be aware of her contributions.

TAKEAWAY:

When times are tough, ensure that you are doing all that you can to add value. Be sure to communicate the value you add in a professional manner either in written updates or in person.

#83

The Tribe Has Spoken—Relating to Those Who Were Voted Out

There is good news and there is bad news. The bad news is that your organization's executive team has announced across-the-board cuts, so a number of employees will be informed that their jobs have been terminated. The good news is that your manager just informed you that you were not selected for the reduction in force because of your consistent contributions and the belief that you will continue to add value in the future.

In such a bad news/good news scenario it can be quite awkward, depressing, or possibly dangerous dealing with those who are affected. In some situations, the affected people are asked to gather their things and leave immediately. Other times, they get notice and have sometimes weeks or possibly months to prepare.

How do you continue to work with affected colleagues? It may not be easy, but you should focus on your responsibilities. That is what your organization compensates you for and is why you are still employed. Granted, depending on the type of relationship you have with each of the affected colleagues, your reactions may vary. If you can focus on your responsibilities, then you will likely continue to be successful, and you can support your departing colleagues to the extent that you want.

Some departing colleagues may attempt to turn you against your organization or engage you in negative conversations. After all, misery loves company. How you feel will depend upon your perception of the process. Were the cuts necessary? How were people informed? Is the organization providing assistance in the form of severance, job placement services, etc.? Is your new role desirable? It is one thing to receive more responsibility, but it is another to have to shoulder the work of two people without any additional recognition in the form of responsibilities, title, or compensation.

If you are let go, remember you are neither the first nor the last person to be laid off. It will hurt, but focus on keeping your confidence up and applying your energy to your new job search. Once you have distanced yourself from the immediate shock, try objectively to evaluate why you were let go.

REAL-LIFE EXAMPLE:

Logan has seen several colleagues depart because of cost-cutting initiatives. He even has had the unfortunate circumstance of having to let go some of the employees who reported to him. Fortunately, all of the departures were amicable, as the organization went to great lengths to make the reductions in force as objective and compassionate as possible. Logan has maintained contact with many of his former colleagues, and they all landed on their feet. Some have even said that their forced departures were a catalyst for improving their careers.

TAKEAWAY:

During challenging times or cutbacks, focus on your responsibilities, and support your less fortunate colleagues through understanding, providing job leads, or acting as a reference.

#84
When Is It Time to Change?

In general, job-hopping will hurt your long-term prospects unless you are in an ultra-competitive field or at the dawn of your career. Does your organization have a demonstrated history of investing in employees and promoting them in responsibilities, title, and benefits? Are there any glass ceilings (e.g., working for a foreign organization that prefers expatriate managers to local managers)?

Moving on makes good sense when the following circumstances are in place:

- Your current organization does not have a demonstrated history of advancing employees in terms of responsibilities, title, or benefits.
- Your current organization has glass ceilings.
- Managers box you in a corner in their minds (e.g., She was an administrative assistant when she started, and she will always be an administrative assistant.).
- Your contributions are not recognized.
- Other companies recruit you to join them.
- A stellar opportunity presents itself.

You need to be the manager of your career. If you are unhappy with your current job and do not foresee change, then it may be time to consider other opportunities. As you move on, try to keep your contacts and leave your current organization gracefully. If you make it an easy transition for your employer, you are more likely to get a good letter of recommendation, maintain favorable relations with others, and maintain a good reputation.

REAL-LIFE EXAMPLE:

Aiden once worked for a foreign-owned organization that unfortunately had a glass ceiling for those not from the home office. Aiden did his best to increase his roles and responsibilities within the organization before deciding to look outside. After three years, Aiden moved to another organization, netting him a significant increase in salary, job responsibilities, and personal satisfaction in the type of work he was doing.

TAKEAWAY:

Sometimes the shortest path to long-term growth is to look outside of your current organization.

PART IV: BONUS TIP—INSIGHTS FOR SUCCESSFUL INTERVIEWS

#85
Maximizing Your Chances for a Successful Interview

You can find many valuable books on job hunting. Rather than try to re-peat all the valuable information available, the following are our thoughts on what matters the most for presenting yourself on paper (i.e., via résumé or curriculum vitae) or in person:

- Selling your potential value to the organization is the most important consideration.
- The "Shark Theory" is crucial—you only need to swim faster than the others to avoid being eaten, so go the extra mile.
- Use your past performance as a predictor of your future performance, including jobs, school work, extracurricular activities like sports, hob-bies, volunteer work, etc.
- Make the connection for the interviewer—tie everything back to how it, directly or indirectly, will translate into your Return on Investment (ROI) if hired.
- Know the organization's products and services—easy to do with the web. We are amazed at how many people who come in for an inter-view appear to have a limited comprehension of our organizations. If the candidates do not take the time to research our organizations, then how can we believe that the candidates are serious (passionate) about joining our organizations?
- Ask intelligent questions, especially about the organization's strategy or how the interviewer got started, for example, to help build rapport.
- You have to prove you are right for the job—no one is entitled to a job. Even if you know that you are a superstar, you will likely give a negative impression if you cross over the line from confident to arrogant.
- Turn nothing into something—everyone has an interesting story, and your interviewer will likely ask you to tell him or her something about yourself. Tell the interviewer a story to engage his or her attention and show how your past experience will benefit the organization.

How successful you are in your interview depends a great deal on the passion you have. If you show that you care about the job and are willing to prepare for the interview, then it sends a strong message that you also will show the same passion in the job. The following is a story shared by James about his first career interview:

Growing up in Southern California, I always hoped that one day I could work at Disneyland® Park. My interview with Disney is a great example of how a little preparation and interesting dialogue can make the difference between being hired or passed over. At the time, Disney was hiring for many different positions, ranging from highly interactive roles (e.g., attractions operator) to behind the scenes kitchen staff at Disneyland Park. Even with many positions to fill, Disney had a well-earned reputation for being highly selective, which meant that only a fraction of applicants would be hired.

My first step in preparation was to ensure that the interviewer knew that I was Disney material. I made sure to use Disney's terminology such as "cast member" instead of "employee" and "attraction" instead of "ride."

As I was only seventeen years old, Disney would not expect that I would bring significant experience to their organization. What they were really concerned with was my potential, as measured by my ability to deliver the guest services for which Disneyland Park was famous. To that end, I set out to make an impression on the interviewer by highlighting several themes, including my lifelong appreciation of and desire to join Disney, my academic accomplishments, and my extracurricular activities.

Within five minutes of the start of the interview, I had made a connection with the interviewer about one of my hobbies, flying. We discovered that we each had a passion for flying and a flying enthusiast's computer game, Flight Simulator (now a Microsoft® product). The fact that I had just completed my evening study of the theories required to obtain a private pilot's license gave the interviewer confidence that I had passion and the ability to learn. I also said that one day if I did not become a professional airline pilot, then I would go into business. The interviewer looked through a list of openings and proposed a cast member position in retailing. It was perfect for me, as it allowed me to learn about retail sales and marketing and interact directly with guests.

Since James' first career interview with Disney, he has tried to establish rapport with those who have interviewed him so that their interviewing job was as easy as possible. As a hiring manager who has interviewed dozens of candidates, James now has a better appreciation of how difficult interviewing someone can be. At times, it feels more like the sort of criminal interrogation depicted in movies, particularly when the candidate is not forthcoming with information.

Even if you have an above average interview, it may be difficult for the interviewer to recall your attributes after he or she has interviewed others. In our experiences, as both candidates and as interviewers, it is important to try to establish a "hook" with the interviewer. This is something that will make you easily remembered, such as the connection that James had with the Disney interviewer.

Some may say that it is be better to be remembered for something that relates directly to the job such as, "Madeline was the candidate who introduced a new partnership that brought her organization $500,000 in additional revenue in three years." In our opinion, you should strive to be remembered for both. Ultimately, you want the interviewer to come away with the following sequence of thoughts:

1. You are a good candidate for the job. For example, "James (preferably, the interviewer is thinking of you now by name) can succeed in all of the job requirements and make a positive contribution to our organization."
2. You have demonstrated your past successes, which points to future successes, and have made an impression on the interviewer. For example, "James is the one who created the five-star partner program for his organization, and he is also the one who has his pilot's license and one day aspires to own his own plane."
3. You should be short-listed as a candidate. For example, "Although our time together was limited, all indicators suggest that James will fit in nicely with our organization's culture."

As soon as possible after an interview, send a follow-up email or hand-written note. The simple fact is that there will be other standout candidates, and some of them are likely to follow up. If you do not follow up, you will not remain at the top of the list. Your follow-up should be based on something you discussed so as to distinguish it from a form letter and to make it easier to recall you. To encourage a response, ask a question that the interviewer can easily answer. This forces a further communication, which reinforces your name recognition; but do not ask something difficult, as you do not want to cost the interviewer time and effort finding an answer.

Even after a mediocre interview, a written or spoken follow-up could be the factor that puts you squarely on the short list for additional interviews, perhaps with a different interviewer or set of interviewers. In essence, your follow-up may be just enough to get an invitation to the next round, where you will have an opportunity to do better than in your previous round.

At the end of the day, if after the interview you still want to be considered for the role, and you think that you have an outside opportunity of winning it, then taking the time to follow up is a minor investment. A handwritten note is still the classiest way to convey appreciation for the interviewer's time, precisely because the interviewer will recognize the investment you will have made. But in some circumstances, you might find that other candidates have locked themselves in for the next round of interviews through instant email follow-ups, and your handwritten note will arrive too late. Our advice is simple: send the handwritten note if you can (if you have good penmanship) in addition to an email and voicemail follow-up.

TAKEAWAY:

Convince your interviewer that you have potential and would bring more benefits to the organization than costs; and do something that will make you memorable after the interviewer has met numerous other applicants, such as delivering a handwritten letter or emailing a follow-up including relevant work samples.

CONCLUSION: TAKEAWAYS

Listed in this section are the 85 tips contained in this book. Some of the tips may have resonated with you so much so that you are eager to implement what you learned; others you may have forgotten as soon as you read them. Circle the ten Takeaways below that you most want to implement over the next thirty days. Do not wait until tomorrow to find ten things you would like to work on—take out your pen now and choose to take action. Reread this list every month, and find ten more to implement until you have integrated each tip into your daily work habits.

Reading a book like this is easy, but changing your habits accordingly takes work and a long-term commitment. Believe us when we write that although these tips are common sense, we have not chosen them lightly. We have encountered these things in our various work experiences. Incorporating these tips *will* help you stand out, *will* help you increase your value to your organization, and *will* increase your chances for success.

#1: Find something you are good at, develop it further, and apply it to your career. You become invaluable to your organization when others recognize your expertise.

#2: Ensure that you are operating against a list of SMART medium- to long-term objectives, and communicate them to those around you to demonstrate your value to your organization. Create short-term SMART goals that will help you achieve your long-term SMART objectives.

#3: Develop a daily list of tasks to focus on and you will increase your productivity toward achieving your goals. Crossing off completed tasks is not only self-satisfying, but it also telegraphs to others that you are a person who knows how to achieve goals.

#4: Save yourself from stress by preparing backup plans. Having a plan B and a plan C prevents commonplace setbacks from becoming disasters.

#5: Arm yourself with data to support your arguments. Even if your arguments do not convince others, you will at least demonstrate your ability to draw conclusions based on underlying data.

#6: Show respect for others by being on time. Build a cushion into your schedule to ensure that you are on time and as relaxed as possible; you can always use the extra time productively at your destination.

#7: Writing counts significantly—even in an era of emails and text messaging.

#8: People respect those who exude confidence, so speak confidently, enunciate carefully, and avoid conditional non-words like *sorta* and *kinda* in your speech.

#9: Becoming a skilled presenter will pay enormous dividends, even if you do not anticipate having to make a formal presentation. The skills you gain will be invaluable in formal presentations as well as in your interactions with people on a daily basis.

#10: Make sure the content of your presentations is memorable by making your content clear, understandable, and easy for your audience to follow. Remember, tell your audience what you are going to tell them, tell them, and then tell them what you told them.

#11: Learn to use spreadsheet applications like Excel to make a positive impression by communicating your data with professional-looking reports and graphs.

#12: Do not mistake action for progress. The key to delivering on time is prioritization—ensure you give yourself enough time to accomplish tasks and allow yourself additional options should you need them.

#13: Keep good records and manage your data so you can answer nearly any question that is asked of you. This ability will show you are knowledgeable and in control of your area of responsibility.

#14: Take a few extra moments to ensure your email communications are polite and respectful, and follow basic rules of professional etiquette.

#15: Save yourself time and stress by getting buy-in ahead of time with relevant people to ensure your plan implementation is smooth and less susceptible to criticism.

#16: When it comes to communications, respect others' time and your organization's money by honing your messages to the essential information.

#17: Be objective and think creatively about all aspects of your job and your organization. Being a problem solver will ensure your manager will not have to be creative when advocating your next raise or promotion!

#18: Develop a critical eye for your own work, and try to deliver more than is expected. By delivering quality, above-and-beyond results, you enhance your value to your organization and create a reputation for yourself as one who delivers.

#19: Developing selling skills, no matter your job description, will benefit you in your job, as you will be better able to convince people to share your point of view.

#20: Change your can-do attitude into a will-do attitude, and hold others accountable to the same standard.

#21: Implement and maintain an open door policy, literally and figuratively, to demonstrate your commitment to teamwork and openness to others.

#22: Show respect for your colleagues, and remember the adage, "What goes around comes around."

#23: Set an example with liberal usage of "please," "thank you," and other gracious words. You will be rewarded with the difference it can make and how others will reciprocate.

#24: Complimenting others has a mutually beneficial effect—make your workplace more pleasant by complimenting at least one person each day.

#25: It may sound cliché, but if you have confidence in yourself, then others will have confidence in you and respect you more, allowing you to be more successful. That is, others will believe in you if you believe in yourself.

#26: Your employer or potential employer does not owe you anything, no matter how successful you have been in the past. Approach all negotiations, whether for a job, a salary raise, a perk, or a bonus, as a matter of proving what you can deliver in the future.

#27: Establish and maintain eye contact with others to show your openness and confidence.

#28: If something bothers you, try to find a way to rectify it. Being proactive about problem solving helps you work better and improves your chances for long-term success. Avoid being labeled a complainer—if this proves too difficult for you, then you will be able to add your lack of advancement to your complaints.

#29: Engaging in gossip can be the start of a slippery slope that could ultimately derail your career—it is best avoided entirely.

#30: Use BCC only when necessary. If an email is important enough for someone to see it, then he or she should be CC'd. However, use CC sparingly, as not everyone needs to be copied on every email.

#31: If anything you post online would come as an embarrassment to you if your colleagues found out or confronted you with it, then consider not posting, and forgo any possibility of being embarrassed.

#32: Humor can relieve stressful situations and lighten the monotony of a day. Use it with discretion to avoid seeming flip and unintentionally offending or hurting the feelings of colleagues.

#33: Treat requests for assistance from others with the same respect and attention to which you would want yours to be treated. Delivering quality in a speedy manner is a fast way to increase your value.

#34: Failure is bound to happen, but always try your very best with the resources you have. Embrace every failure as a learning opportunity, and apply what you have learned toward achieving your next success.

#35: Salespeople often seem to get all the credit and extra perks. Although it does not seem fair to non-sales, non-commissioned personnel, salespeople possess unique skills that require incentives and are critical to an organization's existence.

#36: Be someone that others can count on and earn a reputation as a Clutch Hitter. By helping others, especially your superiors, be more successful, you will be the one others turn to when they need something done properly, quickly, or secretly.

#37: Leverage your accomplishments in other fields, and let the Halo Effect enhance the perception people have of you in your work position.

#38: Meetings are often unnecessary or badly managed, but with minimal effort, you can minimize their impact on your schedule and maximize their effectiveness so that you can achieve your objectives.

#39: Be aware of Time Vampires, as they may suck away your productivity and make you look underworked or unprofessional.

#40: When you admit to a mistake, preferably sooner rather than later, you are actually building trust in you and possibly keeping your organization from suffering worse effects had you kept the mistake concealed.

#41: Your integrity is vital to your success and one asset that cannot be destroyed by others—only you can damage it. Be truthful and protect your integrity.

#42: Keep organization secrets secret. As you advance in your organization, you will be trusted with increasing amounts of confidential information that you have an ethical duty to keep confidential.

#43: A bit of verbal pleasantry costs little but is invaluable. Let people know through your tone that they are important to you. Advise them if you are traveling, and state a goal of responding within one business day—and do it.

#44: Whether you are an individual contributor or a manager, ensure your team shares credit for successes, and if you are a manager, assume responsibility for losses.

#45: When it comes to motivation, a combination of the carrot and stick is likely to be your best approach, as it will motivate many and rid your organization of those who are undeserving.

#46: Realizing one's career aspirations takes a little initiative and support from management. If you are an individual contributor, show how you want to grow. If you are a manager, take an interest in your team members' career goals and help them develop their potentials. Doing this not only makes the team stronger, but it also helps your team perform better.

#47: Managing your manager may empower you to set your own agenda and earn his or her respect, *but* use common sense to ensure that your actions are not (mis)interpreted as coming from a self-promoting or disrespectful subordinate.

#48: If you suspect unethical behavior in your organization and have some corroborating proof to support your suspicions, you should report your suspicions to the appropriate personnel. Respect the anonymity of whistle-blowers and ensure that any future whistle-blowers are not dissuaded from coming forward.

#49: Do not be afraid to toot your own horn. Assume that if you do not do it for yourself, no one else will.

#50: Make it a point to remember others' names as a mark of courtesy and respect.

#51: Being a good follower is a critical skill and will help prepare you to be a better leader.

#52: If you engage in an intra-office relationship, be discreet and aware that if the relationship should end poorly, anything you said or did may become public knowledge around the office and could possibly tarnish your professional reputation.

#53: If a reasonable person would conclude that your productivity exceeds expectations, your organization will probably turn the other way when it comes to occasional web surfing, emailing, instant messaging, or time off for an errand.

#54: Occasional overtime and a will-do attitude may be critical factors for promotion, but chronic overtime suggests a problem with management, processes, and/or your efficiency.

#55: When it comes to your data, protect it and yourself by keeping backups. A current backup in a safe place will help you recover the files you may have lost and get back to work more quickly.

#56: The opportunity for executive interactions should be welcomed as long as you are expert in your area of responsibility, care about the objectives of the organization, and are yourself. You will likely be judged against your peers, so you need not be the smartest, most educated, or best dressed to make a positive impression.

#57: Throughout your career, you will directly or indirectly compete with colleagues for recognition, responsibilities, or promotions, so take the high road and focus on your performance to maximize your opportunities for success.

#58: Use language that is appropriate for your audience, as communication is only possible when the audience receives and understands the intended message.

#59: Packaging yourself includes not only your skills and capabilities but also your outward appearance. Good grooming generally reinforces a person's confidence and makes the person more appealing.

#60: People judge you by the way you dress, especially when they are not privy to your actual work or are shallow. Most likely, they are subconsciously judging you and not even aware of it. Outrageous dress may send an incorrect signal or make others uncomfortable.

#61: A little common "scents" makes a positive impression.

#62: You will do yourself and those around you a favor if you brush your teeth after eating and ensure that your breath is fresh throughout the workday.

#63: Washing your hands is critical to preserving your health, the health of those around you, and maintaining a professional reputation.

#64: Let your handshake introduce you—a firm but friendly grip will convey the type of person you are.

#65: Maintain an organized workspace to make it easier for you to perform your duties. It will also show others that you are in control and effective.

#66: Reading is an investment you make in yourself, whether your reading is for fun or for broadening your knowledge of current events and business acumen. No one who is well-read can ever be accused of being narrow-minded or shortsighted.

#67: Being a compassionate human being is more important than being a success, but if you volunteer outside the office, it may help your professional standing. There are many ways to volunteer, so do what works within your schedule and speaks to your heart.

#68: Developing expertise in fields unrelated to your career can be personally enriching and professionally rewarding.

#69: Aside from the health benefits of being physically fit, know that being in shape will improve others' perceptions of you and being out of shape will hurt others' perceptions of you.

#70: Round out your image by engaging in extra-office sports with colleagues. You may not be a superstar in the office yet, but on the field, even a novice player who takes initiative and practices good sportsmanship demonstrates skills that will translate well back in the office.

#71: Try to keep your business and personal lives separate, but when they do overlap, be discreet about what is organizationally confidential.

#72: Joining industry associations will help you excel in your current role and may even serve as the source of a future career opportunity with another organization.

#73: Take full advantage of your organization's education benefits. You will become more valuable within and outside of your organization, as the knowledge you gain will not only help you in your current role, but it will also help accelerate you to the next stage of your career.

#74: An expat assignment can be highly rewarding, but it is critical that you are aware of the unique challenges you will face, professionally and personally, before you volunteer and move your family overseas.

#75: Apply the concern you show for your personal budget to the spending and revenues of your organization. Any money you save or earn may be spent in better ways, for example, covering the pay raise you have been expecting.

#76: Whether your goal is to increase your job security or be on the fast track to promotion, consider volunteering for additional work or intra-organizational activities.

#77: Intelligently applied, your organization's employee suggestion program can be a great way to add value to your organization, increase your value, and potentially benefit your pocketbook.

#78: Stay close to the money—the more easily identifiable your contribution is to accomplishing your organization's mission, the stronger your job security.

#79: Find a mentor either within or outside your organization. The advice and counsel this person may provide will help you grow in the present and possibly assist you in the future.

#80: Because people are paid on future, not past, performance, continually demonstrate your value to your organization rather than relying on past successes to improve your chances for promotion and insulate you when times get tough.

#81: Employment is a matter of supply and demand. If you put yourself in high demand through consistent, identifiable contributions to your organization, and you respectfully communicate to your organization what your expectations are, then you increase your likelihood of being rewarded.

#82: When times are tough, ensure that you are doing all that you can to add value. Be sure to communicate the value you add in a professional manner either in written updates or in person.

#83: During challenging times or cutbacks, focus on your responsibilities, and support your less fortunate colleagues through understanding, providing job leads, or acting as a reference.

#84: Sometimes the shortest path to long-term growth is to look outside of your current organization.

#85: Convince your interviewer that you have potential and would bring more benefits to the organization than costs; and do something that will make you memorable after the interviewer has met numerous other applicants, such as delivering a handwritten letter or emailing a follow-up including relevant work samples.

ABOUT THE AUTHORS

James J. and Nicole D. Simon have more than twenty-five years of combined experience in organizations ranging from Fortune Magazine's "Best 100 Companies to Work For" to nonprofits. For the past five years, they have been on an expatriate assignment based in Singapore, with James overseeing the marketing in Asia-Pacific for an $800 million high-tech organization. Their experiences in small and large offices, and in U.S.- and foreign-owned companies have helped to shape their knowledge of increasing one's value in an organization and maximizing one's compensation.

James earned his Bachelor of Science in Business Administration from the University of Arizona and his MBA from San Francisco State University. Nicole earned her Bachelor of Arts in history and political science from California State University Fullerton and her MBA from Pepperdine University.

www.ingramcontent.com/pod-product-compliance
Lightning Source LLC
Chambersburg PA
CBHW071428170526
45165CB00001B/437